JOURN

THE PSALMS

JOURNALLING THE PSALMS

A Guide for Reflection and Prayer

Paula Gooder

HODDER &
STOUGHTON

First published in Great Britain in 2022 by Hodder & Stoughton
An Hachette UK company

1

A CIP catalogue record for this title is available from the British Library

Hardback ISBN 978 1 529 38005 7

Typeset in Arno Pro by MPS Limited

Printed and Bound in Great Britain by Clays Ltd, Elcograf S.p.A.

Hodder & Stoughton policy is to use papers that are natural, renewable and recyclable products and made from wood grown in sustainable forests. The logging and manufacturing processes are expected to conform to the environmental regulations of the country of origin.

Hodder & Stoughton Ltd
Carmelite House
50 Victoria Embankment
London EC4Y 0DZ

www.hodderfaith.com

Contents

Introduction

The Psalms contain some of the most beautiful lines in Scripture: lines that inspire and comfort us when we need them most and draw us into a life of prayer and praise. They have been prayed continually for well over 2,000 years. When we pray with the Psalms, we participate in an unbroken chain of daily prayer that stretches back thousands of years, joining with both Jews and Christians who have prayed and sung, praised and lamented, given thanks and mourned using the Psalms every single day, year in and year out. This is not to say that praying the Psalms is easy. They take us on a rollercoaster of emotion, from joy to anguish, from praise to fury, from deep calm to utter torment.

In some ways, praying the Psalms is a communal activity. We may not feel all the emotions contained within a particular Psalm, but we can be sure that someone in our community does. As a result, the Psalms encourage us to pray not just on our own behalf but also on behalf of those around us in our communities, echoing their emotional responses as well as our own. It can help to hold your own community in your mind – or the community of faith around the world – as you pray, knowing that someone, somewhere will be feeling the emotions of the Psalm you are praying, even if, today, you do not. The Psalms remind us of community, of the people around us, known or unknown to us, and all that their lives hold. They also call us to worship and pray together.

The book of Psalms – sometimes called the Psalter – is designed for public worship. Originally the Psalms were sung in the temple itself to accompany the worship there or on the way to the temple by pilgrims. In Christian contexts they have been recited or sung in various different ways, but often corporately. For many years the Psalms were not just the prayer book of the church, they were its hymnbook too.

The Psalms are powerful when said or sung communally, but they are equally powerful when prayed alone, and it is this aspect of the Psalms that is the focus of this journalling book. The book aims to encourage you in your own personal devotions to think more deeply about the Psalms and, in thinking about them, to pray them. It seeks to give you time to reflect on what they seem to be saying generally and then, more specifically, to ask yourself what they might be saying to you or to those around you. There is plenty of space for your own thoughts; use the spaces between the text however works for you, for doodling or drawing, writing or just jotting down words. The questions in the boxes suggest topics or issues you might want to think about, but do feel at liberty to let your thoughts run free; use your imagination as you reflect and see where it leads you. I would also stress that there is no 'right' answer to any question asked – answer as you want to (not answering is also fine!).

Don't forget to sing the Psalms too! As you reflect on them, if you know a tune (or even if you don't), do sing the words. This is how they were prayed in the temple more than two thousand years ago.

When were the Psalms written?

The question of when the Psalms were written is one of the hardest to answer. Most of them range in date from about the ninth century BC to about the fifth century BC, but unless, like Psalm 137, they refer to a particular event in history, it can be hard to be sure about when they were first written. One of the reasons for this is that they have been used – said or sung – day after day, week after week, ever since they were first written. This means that each Psalm has had many contexts – its original context and myriads of contexts ever since. Every time a Psalm fitted perfectly in someone's life or spoke powerfully of someone's experience it gained a new context, a new time and space in which it spoke of and to God. This means that it can be very difficult to work out exactly when any one Psalm was first written, and in some ways it becomes less important too. Every time a Psalm is prayed from the heart, it gains a new author.

Traditionally, the Psalms were attributed to David, who was well known as a composer, singer and poet. Stories in 1 and 2 Samuel tell of him playing the lyre (1 Sam. 16:23), of his singing and dancing (2 Sam. 6:14-22) and of his laments at times of tragedy (2 Sam. 1:17-27). This appears to be supported by the Psalms that have 'of David' in their title (seventy-three Psalms are ascribed to David). The challenge, however, is that not all Psalms do have 'of David'; some have 'of Solomon' (Pss 72; 127) or 'of Asaph' (Pss 50 and 73–83), and some, like Psalm 137, mentioned above, were clearly set long after the time of David.

Over the years, scholars have scratched their heads over the authorship of the Psalms. For a while, many disputed the connection between David and the Psalms, but this picture is now changing. There is such a strong tradition about David's praying, singing and playing of the lyre inspired by God, that it seems reasonable to assume that David was a huge influence on the psalmic tradition, even if he did not write every Psalm. We might want to call him the 'father of the Psalms' – the author of some and the inspiration for others.

What are the titles for?

More than three-quarters of the Psalms (116 out of 150) have titles or superscriptions. As we noted above, some of these appear to indicate either authorship (for example, written by David or Solomon) or inspiration (in the style of David or Solomon). The phrase 'of David' or 'of Solomon' could mean either. (Other names of possible authors or sources of inspiration include Asaph (twelve Psalms); the sons of Korah (eleven Psalms); Moses (one Psalm); Ethan the Ezrahite (one Psalm) and Heman the Ezrahite (one Psalm).

About one-third of the Psalm titles are addressed to the director of music with either an instruction of what instrument to use ('With stringed instruments', Ps. 4, or 'For pipes', Ps. 5) or a suggestion of what tune to play them to ('According to *gittith*', Ps. 81, or 'To the tune of "Lilies"', Ps. 69). Some titles tell us what kind of Psalm it is: 'a *maskil*' (Ps. 53; a *maskil* may have been a meditation or reflection) or 'a *miktam*' (Ps. 56; no one quite knows what a *miktam* is but it might refer to it being 'golden' or special). Occasionally the title tells us what the Psalm was for: 'A wedding song' (Ps. 45), or it associates the Psalm with an occasion in David's life (Ps. 51, 'When the prophet Nathan came to him after David had committed adultery with Bathsheba').

Tempting though it is to skip over the titles of the Psalms, it is worth pausing with them for a moment as they may tell you something you might otherwise miss.

What does *selah* mean?

In some translations you will see the word *selah* interspersed throughout the Psalms. The NIV translation of the Psalms used in this book does not include *selah*, but people are so intrigued by this word that it is worth mentioning here. The problem is that no one is quite clear what the word *selah* means, as it is not used anywhere else in Hebrew. The best guess is that it indicates a musical interlude of some kind – maybe sung or maybe instrumental. If this is true, it is a somewhat intriguing idea. It might point to there being regular points in the Psalms for further reflection on what was being said. This book picks up on that tradition and provides space to reflect on the Psalms as you go.

How were they played or sung?

One feature that comes through clearly from the Psalms is that music was crucially important in their recitation. Psalm 150 is perhaps the best example of this as it lists many of the musical instruments that could be used to praise God. There was singing and dancing aplenty, but they were also accompanied by the blowing of a ram's horn (the *shofar* or trumpet), by stringed instruments (harp, lyre and lute), by wind instruments (the pipes and flutes) and by percussive instruments (tambourine, or timbrel and cymbals). In other words, the singing of Psalms in the temple would have been very noisy indeed!

Should we omit the difficult parts?

Some parts of the Psalms are beautiful, moving and uplifting; other parts are horrifying, blood curdling and visceral. Sometimes it can feel preferable to omit the most difficult verses in public worship, especially if there is no opportunity to explain where they come from and why they are there. In my opinion, however, it is vitally important to include them for personal study/devotion. The Psalms contain the full range of human emotions – even if this range makes us feel profoundly uncomfortable. In prayer we are free to bring to God exactly what we feel, even if we are unable to express that feeling in any other part of our lives. The psalmists did, and so can we. Ensuring that we read the less-seemly verses of the Psalms reminds us of the importance of bringing everything about ourselves into the presence of God, even when – possibly especially when – God feels distant from us.

Journalling the Psalms

Praying the Psalms is a communal activity, but it is also – and always has been – a personal one. Songs like Mary's song (the Magnificat, Luke 1:46-55) and Simeon's song (the Nunc Dimittis, Luke 2:29-32) clearly draw their style and inspiration from the Psalms. This indicates that people would pray and reflect on the Psalms in private and would sometimes write their own to fit their own situation.

This volume invites you to engage with the Psalms personally, but in a slightly different way. Journalling encourages you to write down your thoughts and your feelings, and by doing that to untangle what you really think and feel. The Psalms, with their own jumble of emotions, are a perfect focus for journalling. So often we say or sing a Psalm all the way through and then move on to the next thing we have to do. This volume encourages you to slow down your reading and to think again, about both the full sweep of the Psalm and detailed phrases or words. One of the things that I have found over the years is that if I can read more slowly and reflectively, I can learn so much more about God, about the world and about myself as I read.

The volume contains just fifteen Psalms, but once you have finished it you might like to continue onwards and use what you have learnt from journalling these fifteen when reading the other Psalms in the Psalter.

The book of Psalms is a treasure trove of prayer and praise. While researching for this guided journal I asked my social media followers to tell me which Psalms had been the most important in their journey of faith. The fifteen Psalms that follow are a representative selection and deliberately illustrate the full range of Psalms, from those full of praise through those full of lament to those that look back on harrowing experiences to trace God's presence through it all. My prayer is that in reflecting on them, you will become ever more infused with a confidence in God's loving presence through the joys and sorrows of life.

Psalm 1

....

Psalm 1 isn't only the first of the Psalms, it may also
be an introduction to the whole book. In fact, in a few early
editions of the Psalms, Psalm 1 is placed before the rest, on its
own and without a number, so that it acts as a preface to what
follows. One reason for this is that Psalm 1 has no title, unlike
the majority of the Psalms. This raises the question of whether
Psalm 1 is itself the title for the whole of the Psalter, telling us
how to read and pray what follows.

Psalm 1 introduces the idea that there are two ways of living:
one way leads to blessing and the other to judgement; one
way leads to a life that is rooted and secure and the other to an
ephemeral existence that can be blown away by a gust of wind.
The implication of the Psalm is that if you want to know more
you should read, pray or sing all of the Psalms that follow.

 **Read the Psalm slowly. What words or phrases jump
out at you?**

Psalm 1

[1] Blessed is the one
  who does not walk in step with the wicked
 or stand in the way that sinners take
  or sit in the company of mockers,
[2] but whose delight is in the law of the LORD,
  and who meditates on his law day and night.
[3] That person is like a tree planted by streams of water,
  which yields its fruit in season
 and whose leaf does not wither –
  whatever they do prospers.

[4] Not so the wicked!
  They are like chaff
  that the wind blows away.
[5] Therefore the wicked will not stand in the judgment,
  nor sinners in the assembly of the righteous.

[6] For the LORD watches over the way of the righteous,
  but the way of the wicked leads to destruction.

STANDING BACK
Looking at the whole Psalm

The Psalm falls into four rough parts based on the contrast between the blessed and the wicked: the two sections at the start are longer and the two at the end much shorter.

- Verses 1-3 talk about 'the blessed' – what they are like and what will happen to them.

- Verse 4-5 talk about 'the wicked' and what will happen to them.

- The first line of verse 6 reflects on why the righteous are as they are (because God watches over them).

- The second line of verse 6 states the fate of the wicked.

TO THINK ABOUT . . .

The Psalm is set up as a contrast between the blessed and the wicked but, if you look closely, you will see the four sections don't match, the description of the blessed doesn't follow the same pattern as that for the wicked. What do you think the main differences are?

The writer of this Psalm believes that good things will happen to those who love God. As we all know, life itself reveals that this is not always the case and, as the book of Job makes clear, sometimes bad things do happen to good people. The picture the psalmist uses here, however, is interesting; it reminds me of Jesus' parable about the wise and foolish builders – your foundations (or, as in this Psalm, 'roots') really are important in difficult times.

SPACE TO DOODLE

Where are your roots? How confident are you that they will hold when the storms come?

QUITE INTERESTING

Psalm 1 begins with the first letter of the Hebrew alphabet and ends with its last letter. This implies it covers the whole of life from A to Z or, as in Hebrew, from *aleph* to *taw*.

ZOOMING IN
Picking up some details

'Blessed' (verse 1)

There are two words for 'blessed' in Hebrew: the one used here (*ašrē*) and one used to describe what priests do in the temple (*baruk*). People often translate the word used here as 'happy', to make it clear it is not the blessing that priests give in the temple. The problem is that 'happy' is not big or satisfying enough to convey all that is meant by *ašrē*. 'Happy' implies a somewhat superficial contentment with a life that goes well.

> **TO THINK ABOUT ...**
> Think about the word 'blessed' – jot down all the different words that 'blessed' suggests to you.

'The one' (verse 1)

Although it is harder to see in English, it is important to notice that the Psalm refers to the person who is blessed in the singular ('the one'; the Hebrew actually says 'the man') but the wicked in the plural ('they'). This suggests that 'the righteous' may feel overwhelmed and outnumbered by 'the wicked' that surround them.

TO THINK ABOUT . . .

Have you ever felt overwhelmed/outnumbered by those who have different values or morals from you? What did it feel like? Then think about the image of being a tree with deep roots. Does this change anything?

'Walk . . . stand . . . sit' (verse 1)

Notice the verbs used to describe what a righteous person does not do. The suggestion seems to be one of progression: first you try it out by walking it, then you get used to it and stand in it and finally you sit down in it and it becomes a habit.

SPACE TO DOODLE

Think about the image of walking, standing and sitting in the way of the wicked/sinners/mockers – does it ring a bell for you in any way?

QUITE INTERESTING

The word translated 'meditate' probably means to say out loud, as people in the ancient world did not read silently. The same verb is used elsewhere to refer to the cooing of pigeons (Isa. 38:14), the growling of a lion (Isa. 31:4) and the voice of a human being (Ps. 35:28).

A tree by a river (verse 3)

The image of a tree planted by a river is one of the most striking and effective in all of the Psalms. The point is that you can't see the nourishment that is given to the tree; you can only see its effect. It is also long term. A tree doesn't develop strong roots overnight; only after days and weeks and months and years of regular nourishment does the tree grow strong and tall, so that when the hard, baking summer comes (as it does in the Holy Land) the tree does not wither away. In the same way, immersing yourself in the word of God is something that no one else can see, but its effects over a long period of time will give you strength when you need it most.

SPACE TO DOODLE

Think about the tree by the river drinking in nourishment. Where does the image take you in your thinking?

- A reminder of the long-distance nature of the Christian life.

- There are also seasons to life.
  - plenty v. drought
  - fruit + no fruit (produce)
- fruit of being still exist

'Like chaff' (verse 4)

Notice the difference between those whose roots are deep in
the law of the Lord and those who are like chaff. In the ancient
world, the process of wind winnowing prepared wheat for
grinding. A wooden winnowing fork would be used to throw
grains of wheat into the air, the chaff (the dry, scaly outer part
of the grain) would blow away in the wind and the heavier inner
kernel would fall back to the ground.

TO THINK ABOUT . . .

Why might the psalmist claim that the wicked are blown
away like chaff?

'The LORD watches over' (verse 6)

This last verse is the focus of the whole Psalm. It is the first time that God is mentioned directly (in verse 2 the law of the Lord is mentioned but not God specifically), and here the real contrast at play throughout the Psalm is revealed between the way of the righteous and the way of the wicked. The way of the righteous is watched over by a caring and loving God; the way of the wicked is independent and autonomous but leads in one direction – to destruction.

TO THINK ABOUT . . .

What do you think it means for God to watch over the way of the righteous?

Now go back and read the Psalm again slowly. Make a note this time of the words that you notice. Are they the same or have they changed? As you finish your reflection on the Psalm, you might like to ask yourself three questions:

- How did it make me feel?

- What did it make me think about?

- What do I now need to pray for/about?

Psalm 22

....

For Christians, Psalm 22 is best known for containing
Jesus' cry from the cross '"*Eli, Eli, lema sabachthani?*" which
means "My God, my God, why have you forsaken me?"' (Matt.
27:46; Mark 15:34). This is not the only reference to this Psalm
in the crucifixion accounts: verses 7-8 ('All who see me mock
me . . .'), verse 15 ('my mouth is dried up like a potsherd'), verse
16 ('they pierce my hands and my feet') and verse 18 ('they
cast lots for my garment') all resonate with events from the
crucifixion. It is interesting to read the story of the crucifixion
(especially Mark's version, 15:21-41) next to Psalm 22 and to
note how they relate to each other.

Psalm 22 is a powerful example of how Jesus used the
Psalms, but it should also be read in its own right as a
remarkable interweaving of despair and praise, an interweaving
that goes backwards and forwards throughout the Psalm until it
ends in a statement of great hope and confidence in the future.

 **Read the Psalm slowly. What words or phrases jump
out at you?**

Psalm 22

For the director of music. To the tune of 'The Doe of the Morning'. A psalm of David.

¹ My God, my God, why have you forsaken me?
    Why are you so far from saving me,
    so far from my cries of anguish?
² My God, I cry out by day, but you do not answer,
    by night, but I find no rest.

³ Yet you are enthroned as the Holy One;
    you are the one Israel praises.
⁴ In you our ancestors put their trust;
    they trusted and you delivered them.
⁵ To you they cried out and were saved;
    in you they trusted and were not put to shame.

⁶ But I am a worm and not a man,
    scorned by everyone, despised by the people.
⁷ All who see me mock me;
    they hurl insults, shaking their heads.
⁸ 'He trusts in the LORD,' they say,
    'let the LORD rescue him.
  Let him deliver him,
    since he delights in him.'

⁹ Yet you brought me out of the womb;
    you made me trust in you, even at my mother's
        breast.
¹⁰ From birth I was cast on you;
    from my mother's womb you have been my God.

¹¹ Do not be far from me,
    for trouble is near
    and there is no one to help.

¹² Many bulls surround me;
　　strong bulls of Bashan encircle me.
¹³ Roaring lions that tear their prey
　　open their mouths wide against me.
¹⁴ I am poured out like water,
　　and all my bones are out of joint.
　My heart has turned to wax;
　　it has melted within me.
¹⁵ My mouth is dried up like a potsherd,
　　and my tongue sticks to the roof of my mouth;
　　you lay me in the dust of death.

¹⁶ Dogs surround me,
　　a pack of villains encircles me;
　　they pierce my hands and my feet.
¹⁷ All my bones are on display;
　　people stare and gloat over me.
¹⁸ They divide my clothes among them
　　and cast lots for my garment.

¹⁹ But you, Lord, do not be far from me.
　　You are my strength; come quickly to help me.
²⁰ Deliver me from the sword,
　　my precious life from the power of the dogs.
²¹ Rescue me from the mouth of the lions;
　　save me from the horns of the wild oxen.

²² I will declare your name to my people;
　　in the assembly I will praise you.
²³ You who fear the Lord, praise him!
　　All you descendants of Jacob, honour him!
　　Revere him, all you descendants of Israel!
²⁴ For he has not despised or scorned
　　the suffering of the afflicted one;
　he has not hidden his face from him
　　but has listened to his cry for help.

25 From you comes the theme of my praise in the great
    assembly;
  before those who fear you I will fulfil my vows.
26 The poor will eat and be satisfied;
  those who seek the LORD will praise him –
  may your hearts live for ever!

27 All the ends of the earth
    will remember and turn to the LORD,
  and all the families of the nations
    will bow down before him,
28 for dominion belongs to the LORD
    and he rules over the nations.

29 All the rich of the earth will feast and worship;
    all who go down to the dust will kneel before him –
    those who cannot keep themselves alive.
30 Posterity will serve him;
    future generations will be told about the Lord.
31 They will proclaim his righteousness,
    declaring to a people yet unborn:
    He has done it!

STANDING BACK
Looking at the whole Psalm

We noted in the introduction that Psalm 22 weaves together despair and praise throughout the Psalm. Look first at verses 1-21 and notice how they move backwards and forwards between despair and trust (verses 1-2 then 3-5; 6-8 then 9-11; 12-21 then 22-31).

TO THINK ABOUT . . .

Spend some time thinking about this movement from despair to trust and back again. Why do you think the psalmist does this?

Notice the abrupt change in the tone of the Psalm between verse 21 and 22. Something has clearly happened to change everything for the author. As with all of the Psalms, we can't know what happened that changed how the psalmist felt; all we have left is the change in emotion, tone and outlook.

TO THINK ABOUT . . .

Look at this change – notice the difference in how the psalmist saw the world from verses 1-21 and then from 22-31. Maybe what changed wasn't just what was going on but how the psalmist felt about it. Have you ever experienced something similar, when nothing changed but you just felt differently about a situation?

QUITE INTERESTING

When Jesus quoted the Psalm in the Gospels he quoted it in Aramaic, the everyday language he spoke, not in Hebrew, the formal religious language that would normally have been used for Scripture.

ZOOMING IN
Picking up some details

'Why have you forsaken me?' (verse 1)

There is a reason that the cry at the start of the Psalm is so well known. There is something about the agony summed up in the words that communicates the utter despair that we all sometimes feel.

QUITE INTERESTING

Although 'cries of anguish' (v.1) is a more elegant translation, the Hebrew actually says 'roaring words', which communicates a little more of the visceral emotion expressed by the writer here.

SPACE TO DOODLE

Spend time reflecting on the cry, 'Why have you forsaken me?' Do you think God had actually forsaken the psalmist?

'So far from saving me' (verse 1)

One of the themes that runs throughout this Psalm is that of God's absence and presence. The psalmist feels abandoned by God and begs God not to be so far away.

TO THINK ABOUT . . .

Trace this theme through the Psalm, jotting down the key phrases as you go, noting hints of God's absence and pleas for God's presence. Have you ever felt that God has abandoned you? What phrases resonate with you most?

'Scorned by everyone' (verse 6)

The problem is not just that the psalmist feels that God has abandoned him but also that the people around him are bullying and threatening him.

> **TO THINK ABOUT . . .**
>
> Again, trace this theme through the Psalm, noting the language the psalmist uses to describe how others treat him.

QUITE INTERESTING

The Hebrew word translated as 'worm' in verse 6 refers to either a worm or a grub. At the time, worms and grubs were associated with destroying plants or consuming corpses. So a better modern translation might be a maggot. The word refers to something that had no value at all.

Bones, heart, mouth, tongue (verses 14-15)

Notice the physicality of the psalmist's despair. He feels it in his bones, his heart, his mouth and his tongue – not to mention being 'poured out like water'.

SPACE TO DOODLE

Think about the imagery he uses to describe how he feels – what language would you use to describe how your body feels during the darkest times of life. What body parts would you point to and what language would you associate with them?

QUITE INTERESTING

Notice that in addition to dedicating this Psalm to the director of music and connecting it with David, this Psalm notes the tune to which it should be sung ('The Doe of the Morning'). Unfortunately, although we know that the Psalms were sung and were accompanied by instruments like the harp and the lyre, very little is known about what the tunes were like.

'I will declare your name' (verse 22)

When the psalmist feels abandoned by God, he feels entirely
alone as well. He sees everyone as enemies who are against him.
From verse 22 onwards he is surrounded by people with whom
he is keen to share the good news of his salvation.

TO THINK ABOUT . . .

Jot down the people and groups of people mentioned
from verse 22 onwards and reflect on the difference you
notice between this and the earlier part of the Psalm.

'He has done it!' (verse 31)

The Psalm ends with a shout of triumph that contrasts powerfully with the cry of despair at the beginning. It has journeyed from, 'My God, my God, why have you forsaken me?' to, 'He has done it!' The full range of human emotion is held together in this single Psalm, from darkest despair to glorious joy and hope.

TO THINK ABOUT . . .

Christian communities tend to be better at the 'He has done it!' expression of emotion than at the 'My God, my God why have you forsaken me?' kind. What sorts of things might we do that would take people's despair and grief seriously?

Now go back and read the Psalm again slowly. Make a note this time of the words that you notice. Are they the same or have they changed? As you finish your reflection on the Psalm, you might like to ask yourself three questions:

- How did it make me feel?
- What did it make me think about?
- What do I now need to pray for/about?

....
....
....
....
....
....
....
....
....
....
....
....
....
....
....
....
....
....
....
....

Psalm 23

Psalm 23 is one of the best known of all the Psalms, and the fact that it has been set to so many different tunes probably makes it the most sung and prayed of them all too. It might even be the best-loved Psalm, though there are a number that fall into this category. At first glance it is a simple Psalm that brings to mind green fields, fluffy white sheep and a gentle shepherd. These images are present but, if you look again, you realise that there is much more going on: danger lurks all around and the shepherd protects the sheep from those who threaten it (as well as throwing a banquet at the end). This is a Psalm that expresses profound trust in the Lord who cares for us and guides us, but it is also a Psalm that takes seriously the difficult times in life – times when the way is hard and the valley is at its darkest.

 Read the Psalm slowly. What words or phrases jump out at you?

Psalm 23
A psalm of David

[1] The LORD is my shepherd, I lack nothing.
[2]   He makes me lie down in green pastures,
  he leads me beside quiet waters,
[3]   he refreshes my soul.
  He guides me along the right paths
    for his name's sake.
[4] Even though I walk
    through the darkest valley,
  I will fear no evil,
    for you are with me;
  your rod and your staff,
    they comfort me.

[5] You prepare a table before me
    in the presence of my enemies.
  You anoint my head with oil;
    my cup overflows.
[6] Surely your goodness and love will follow me
    all the days of my life,
  and I will dwell in the house of the LORD
    for ever.

STANDING BACK
Looking at the whole Psalm

The first thing to notice is that there are in fact two key themes in the Psalm, not just 'The LORD is my shepherd' – the one we normally remember. The theme changes halfway through:

- Verses 1-4 reflect on God as shepherd.

- Verses 5-6 reflect on God as a generous host who throws his guest a huge feast.

TO THINK ABOUT . . .

How do the themes of God as shepherd and host relate to each other? Why do you think the psalmist moved from one to the other?

Notice also that the psalmist changes the pronouns he uses for God halfway through.

- In verses 1-3 God is referred to in the third person: 'The Lord is . . . he makes me . . . he leads me . . . he refreshes'.

- and then in the middle of verse 4 the pronoun changes to 'you': 'you are with me . . . your rod . . . you prepare . . .'

SPACE TO DOODLE

Sit and feel the difference between the first part of the Psalm and the second part, between the speaking about God and the speaking to God.

ZOOMING IN
Picking up some details

The Lord as shepherd (verse 1)

In the Bible, God is often described as a shepherd, especially in the Psalms: like this, 'Hear us, Shepherd of Israel, you who lead Joseph like a flock' (Ps. 80:1), or, 'Know that the LORD is God. It is he who made us, and we are his; we are his people, the sheep of his pasture' (Ps. 100:3).

Shepherds were and are a common sight in the Holy Land. Early in the morning they are often seen leading their flocks out of the village in search of small patches of grass in the dry and scrubby landscape. Shepherds and their sheep can conjure a gentle image for us of green grass and long summer days, but for shepherds in the ancient world, the reality was much harsher than that. Grass was often scarce, and flocks were circled by predators both on the ground and in the air. The shepherd's job was not just to find grass for their sheep but also to beat off the wild animals and vultures that followed their every step.

TO THINK ABOUT . . .

What does it feel like to imagine God as fearless defender of sheep from predators?

'The LORD shepherds me' (verse 1)

Although most versions of this Psalm translate the opening phrase as 'The LORD is my shepherd', the Hebrew actually uses a verb instead of a noun, so the literal translation would be something along the lines of, 'The LORD shepherds me or feeds me or drives me to pasture or protects or nourishes me.' In other words, God acts towards us as a shepherd would towards the flock.

SPACE TO DOODLE If the opening verse says, 'The LORD shepherds me . . .', does this change the way you see God? If so, how?

How does the Lord shepherd us? (verses 1-2)

The Psalm identifies five things that the Lord does as a shepherd:

- makes sure I am not deprived of anything that I need ('I lack nothing');

- provides me with a place for nourishment and rest ('makes me lie down in green pastures');

- gives me rest that is free from danger – the Hebrew word doesn't just mean quiet; it refers to the kind of rest that comes from knowing you are completely safe ('leads me beside quiet waters');

- provides deep refreshment that makes me feel alive again ('refreshes my soul');

- leads me along the best route that I can take ('guides me along the right paths').

TO THINK ABOUT . . .

Spend time reflecting on these five actions of God. Think of a time in your life when you were aware of each one.

The dark valley (verse 4)

Verse four rescues this Psalm from being too trite. God does shepherd us through good times but also in the worst of times. Notice that it is at verse 4 that the pronoun changes from 'he' to 'you'. It is during the darkest times that God's presence is most keenly felt, the relationship experienced most deeply.

The word translated 'comfort' is also important. This comfort doesn't just say, 'There, there, everything will be alright,' but provides courage to face the mortal danger in God's presence.

The word 'comfort' has changed meaning over the years and now we associate it with compassion and care. Historically, however, the word's meaning has been much closer to 'courage'. The Latin root behind our word is com (with) + fortis (strength), so conveyed the sense 'give strength to'.

QUITE INTERESTING

The word translated 'darkest' is a fascinating one and can mean 'death-shadow', a time of mortal danger. 'Darkest' half captures it, but we haven't got an English word that quite communicates the danger implied by the Hebrew. Notice that it is God's presence that makes all the difference – 'you are with me'. It doesn't make the danger any less dangerous, but God's presence makes it bearable.

TO THINK ABOUT . . .

Reflect on this image. In the midst of the deepest and darkest danger, God's presence brings courage. Have you experienced this?

A banqueting table (verses 5-6)

It is hard to tell with verses 5-6 whether the psalmist is making the same point again just with a different metaphor or whether the banquet takes the idea further. There is nourishment ('you prepare a table'), protection from danger ('in the presence of my enemies') and extravagance ('my cup overflows'), but there is something more as well.

The first phrase of verse 6 is significant. The psalmists report being followed or pursued by their enemies on multiple occasions. Here, however, it is not the enemies who are chasing them, but goodness and steadfast, never-ending love. God doesn't stay with us only through the hard times but also pursues us with love throughout our lives.

SPACE TO DOODLE Think about the image of being pursued by God's love. When have you tried to avoid God's love and why?

Now go back and read the Psalm again slowly. Make a note this time of the words that you notice. Are they the same or have they changed? As you finish your reflection on the Psalm, you might like to ask yourself three questions:

- How did it make me feel?

- What did it make me think about?

- What do I now need to pray for/about?

Psalm 40

In some ways, Psalm 40 is like Psalm 22, since it weaves together statements of thanksgiving and trust about who God is with a plea for help. Where it is different is *how* it weaves them together. In Psalm 22 the psalmist moves backwards and forwards from plea to trust and back again. This Psalm has two key blocks: verses 1-10, which give thanks for the God who hears and answers prayer, and verses 11-17, which beg God to bring salvation quickly. As a result, the balance of these two Psalms is different. Psalm 22 emerges out of utter despair and clings to trust in the midst of that despair; this Psalm begins in thanksgiving and in trust prays for help. This reminds us that we grieve and lament in different ways at different times in our lives. When we identify Psalms as Psalms of lament or of thanksgiving it is easy to imagine that they are uniform categories: 'happy Psalms' and 'sad Psalms'. The reality is that our joys and sorrows take many different forms, and the Psalms, as true chronicles of human emotion, reflect this variety.

 Read the Psalm slowly. What words or phrases jump out at you?

Psalm 40

For the director of music. Of David. A psalm.

¹ I waited patiently for the LORD;
    he turned to me and heard my cry.
² He lifted me out of the slimy pit,
    out of the mud and mire;
  he set my feet on a rock
    and gave me a firm place to stand.
³ He put a new song in my mouth,
    a hymn of praise to our God.
  Many will see and fear the LORD
    and put their trust in him.

⁴ Blessed is the one
    who trusts in the LORD,
  who does not look to the proud,
    to those who turn aside to false gods.
⁵ Many, LORD my God,
    are the wonders you have done,
    the things you planned for us.
  None can compare with you;
    were I to speak and tell of your deeds,
    they would be too many to declare.

⁶ Sacrifice and offering you did not desire –
    but my ears you have opened –
    burnt offerings and sin offerings you did not
      require.
⁷ Then I said, 'Here I am, I have come –
    it is written about me in the scroll.
⁸ I desire to do your will, my God;
    your law is within my heart.'

⁹ I proclaim your saving acts in the great assembly;
    I do not seal my lips, LORD,
    as you know.
¹⁰ I do not hide your righteousness in my heart;
    I speak of your faithfulness and your saving help.
  I do not conceal your love and your faithfulness
    from the great assembly.

¹¹ Do not withhold your mercy from me, LORD;
    may your love and faithfulness always protect me.
¹² For troubles without number surround me;
    my sins have overtaken me, and I cannot see.
  They are more than the hairs of my head,
    and my heart fails within me.
¹³ Be pleased to save me, LORD;
    come quickly, LORD, to help me.

¹⁴ May all who want to take my life
    be put to shame and confusion;
  may all who desire my ruin
    be turned back in disgrace.
¹⁵ May those who say to me, 'Aha! Aha!'
    be appalled at their own shame.
¹⁶ But may all who seek you
    rejoice and be glad in you;
  may those who long for your saving help always say,
    'The LORD is great!'

¹⁷ But as for me, I am poor and needy;
    may the Lord think of me.
  You are my help and my deliverer;
    you are my God, do not delay.

STANDING BACK
Looking at the whole Psalm

Although Psalm 40 has two obvious sections, when you look a little closer you can see that, in fact, there are three:

- Verses 1-3: a statement of thanksgiving and trust that the psalmist waited for God. God heard him and gave him a new song to sing.

- Verses 4-10: the new song that the psalmist sang.

- Verses 11-17: a new crisis emerges and the psalmist begs for help.

TO THINK ABOUT . . .

What song are you singing to God at the moment? Is it a new song or an old one?

The audience for this Psalm changes around verse 5. The opening verses imagine the psalmist telling a human audience about everything that God has done, but then he turns and addresses God directly.

TO THINK ABOUT . . .

Can you think of any hymns or worship songs that change their audience? What effect does that change have on you as you sing? How does thinking about that affect how you relate to this Psalm?

ZOOMING IN
Picking up some details

'I waited patiently' (verse 1)

It is quite hard to translate the opening verbs of Psalm 40 into helpful English. Translators usually say, 'I waited patiently,' but the Hebrew says literally, 'Waiting, I waited.' So perhaps a better translation might be, 'I waited and waited' – there is nothing to suggest the waiting was patient. More accurately, the wording implies that the psalmist waited eagerly for God.

SPACE TO DOODLE

Is there a difference between waiting patiently and waiting eagerly? What qualities might each have? What are you waiting for at the moment? What words would you use to describe your waiting?

'He ... heard my cry' (verse 1)

The point that lies at the heart of these opening verses is that the psalmist has previously waited for God and God heard his cry. Therefore he is confident that God will do so again.

TO THINK ABOUT ...

Think back to times when God has felt particularly close or has answered your prayers. If you were to write something similar to the opening verses of Psalm 40, what would you say?

'Many . . . are the wonders you have done' (verse 5)

From verse 5 onwards, the psalmist turns and talks to God. The 'new song' that he sings (verse 3) is quite generic, talking about all God's wonders – in other words, not just what God has done for the psalmist but everything that God has done in the world.

SPACE TO DOODLE

Following on from the last reflection, move as the psalmist does from the particular (what God has done for you) to the general (all the wonders God has done in the world). Write the next lines of your song here.

QUITE INTERESTING

The phrasing of verse 7 is a little odd, and there are various views about what 'the scroll' might be. The two main ones are that the scroll is the equivalent of the book of life mentioned at various points in the Old and New Testaments, or that it is this song of thanksgiving that has been written down and preserved.

'Here I am, I have come' (verse 7)

The phrase, 'Here I am,' is reminiscent of what Isaiah says when God asks who he should send, and Isaiah responds, 'Here am I. Send me!' (Isa. 6:8). In the context of this Psalm, the psalmist's response is similar. God has said what he does not require (verse 6) and the psalmist responds, 'Here I am; I have come . . . I desire to do your will.' The psalmist is wholehearted in his response to God, fully and wholly present.

SPACE TO DOODLE

When you pray the words, 'Here I am, I have come . . . I desire to do your will,' what comes to your mind? Do you feel excited or frightened? Is there anything that stops you saying this at the moment?

QUITE INTERESTING

The English 'Aha' is the closest we can get to the Hebrew *heach* used in verse 15. It was an expression of joy and clearly is meant to communicate the glee the psalmist's enemies felt at the mess he was in.

'Troubles without number surround me' (verse 12)

Notice the language that describes the psalmist's current troubles: they 'surround me'; they 'have overtaken me'. The image suggests the idea of being chased by troubles and them finally catching up with him again.

The psalmist goes on to describe what this feels like and, as in Psalm 22, the language he chooses is very physical: 'I cannot see'; 'they are more than the hairs of my head'; 'my heart fails within me'. It captures very well the sensations – both emotional and bodily – that we feel when we are overwhelmed and terrified by what is happening around us.

TO THINK ABOUT . . .

What imagery would you use to describe your troubles (whether present or in the past)?

'You are my help and my deliverer' (verse 17)

Notice the different feel between the psalmist's slightly desperate 'You are my help and my deliverer' in verse 17 and 'he turned to me and heard my cry' in verse 1. At the start of the Psalm the psalmist is confident and assured; at the end desperate and pleading, but in both situations he is confident in the God who loves and saves him.

SPACE TO DOODLE

Spend some time contemplating these two differing statements of confidence in God – both are equally valid. Do you feel more like the psalmist of verse 1 or verse 17 at the moment?

Now go back and read the Psalm again slowly. Make a note this time of the words that you notice. Are they the same or have they changed? As you finish your reflection on the Psalm, you might like to ask yourself three questions:

- How did it make me feel?

- What did it make me think about?

- What do I now need to pray for/about?

Psalm 42

Psalm 42 opens the second collection in the book of Psalms, which runs from this Psalm all the way through to Psalm 72. Psalm 42 sets up one of the key themes of this particular collection – a longing for God. Many of the psalmists reflect on this theme and what it means in their lives. Book 2 of the Psalter is sometimes known as the Elohistic Psalter because God is addressed in Psalms 42–72 not as *YHWH* (the usual name for God which in English is normally translated as 'Lord'), but as *Elohim*, normally translated 'God'. This is not to say that you will not see 'Lord' in these Psalms, but you will see 'God' (or sometimes 'Lord God') more often than you would normally.

Psalms 42 and 43 are sometimes presented as a single Psalm (though here we will be looking just at 42) because of the refrain, 'Why, my soul, are you downcast?', which occurs in both Psalms. This refrain is particularly striking in that it represents an inner conversation about how to live in difficult times.

 Read the Psalm slowly. What words or phrases jump out at you?

Psalm 42

For the director of music. A maskil *of the Sons of Korah.*

¹ As the deer pants for streams of water,
    so my soul pants for you, my God.
² My soul thirsts for God, for the living God.
    When can I go and meet with God?
³ My tears have been my food
    day and night,
while people say to me all day long,
    'Where is your God?'
⁴ These things I remember
    as I pour out my soul:
how I used to go to the house of God
    under the protection of the Mighty One
with shouts of joy and praise
    among the festive throng.

⁵ Why, my soul, are you downcast?
    Why so disturbed within me?
Put your hope in God,
    for I will yet praise him,
    my Saviour and my God.

⁶ My soul is downcast within me;
    therefore I will remember you
from the land of the Jordan,
    the heights of Hermon – from Mount Mizar.
⁷ Deep calls to deep
    in the roar of your waterfalls;
all your waves and breakers
    have swept over me.

⁸ By day the L<small>ORD</small> directs his love,
   at night his song is with me –
   a prayer to the God of my life.

⁹ I say to God my Rock,
   'Why have you forgotten me?
  Why must I go about mourning,
   oppressed by the enemy?'
¹⁰ My bones suffer mortal agony
   as my foes taunt me,
  saying to me all day long,
   'Where is your God?'

¹¹ Why, my soul, are you downcast?
   Why so disturbed within me?
  Put your hope in God,
   for I will yet praise him,
   my Saviour and my God.

STANDING BACK
Looking at the whole Psalm

This Psalm contains two major sections of lament (verses 1-4 and 6-10) interspersed with a refrain that is repeated (verses 5 and 11). What is unusual about this Psalm is that it is in the two refrains that the lament lightens; there are no other statements of trust or thanksgiving in the Psalm.

TO THINK ABOUT . . .

Reflect on the impact of the two refrains in this Psalm of lament. Do they affect how you read the lament sections? In what way?

Water is a key image that runs through the two major lament sections in Psalm 42, from the yearning for refreshing streams of water to the terrifying deep of the sea.

SPACE TO DOODLE

Trace the use of water through the Psalm, jotting down the range of different words used for it. Reflect on the positive and negative images of water used. What does water represent in each instance?

ZOOMING IN
Picking up some details

'A *maskil* of the Sons of Korah'

The title of this Psalm tells us two things:

- it is connected to the Sons of Korah or Korahites;
- it is a *maskil*.

Numbers 26:58 and 1 Chronicles 9:17-19 tell us that the Korahites were one of the major Levitical families whose roles were as temple assistants (temple musicians, porters and guards). Korah himself is recorded as questioning Moses and Aaron's authority in Numbers 16, but this does not seem to have affected the reputation of his descendants, as this Psalm testifies. It certainly makes sense that there were temple musicians who were writing and producing Psalms to be used in worship. Other Korahite Psalms are 44–9; 84–5; 87–8.

The word *maskil* is connected to the idea of pondering or giving attention to something.

TO THINK ABOUT . . .

This Psalm is a contemplation or a moment of pondering about something. What is it encouraging you to think about?

'As the deer pants for streams of water' (verse 1)

The type of deer referred to in this Psalm was probably Persian fallow deer, which used to roam wild in Israel until their extinction at the end of the nineteenth century (they have recently been reintroduced successfully back into the wild). In the hot Middle-Eastern summers, wild animals really would have panted for water like this. It's a powerful image to describe our need for God when he feels absent.

SPACE TO DOODLE

Reflect on the image of a wild deer panting for water on a hot day. Have you ever felt this kind of longing in your walk with God? What words or phrases describe your longing for God?

QUITE INTERESTING

The word translated as 'soul' in verses 5 and 11 is the Hebrew word *nephesh* and refers to that which brings us life, our life force.

'I used to go to the house of God' (verse 4)

Although, as with many of the Psalms, we don't know anything about the context – and here, we don't know what was preventing the psalmist from going to the temple – many people wonder whether this Psalm is to be read alongside Psalm 137 ('By the rivers of Babylon we sat and wept when we remembered Zion'). Perhaps this is another example of a Psalm that reflects the distress and horror caused by the exile to Babylon in the sixth century BC.

For the Israelites, the temple was an especially important location, a place where they could be close to God. Indeed, for many, the temple was the gateway to heaven itself.

TO THINK ABOUT . . .

For Christians, sacred space is different from the understanding we see here. We can worship God outside sacred buildings, and yet for some, though not for all, buildings are a vital part of their worship experience. What does sacred space mean for you and your worshipping life?

'Why, my soul, are you downcast?' (verses 5 and 11)

One of the most striking features of the refrain, which is repeated, is the inner conversation it describes. In some ways it feels a more modern way of imagining the self. The psalmist has two competing voices within: one that is despairing and hopeless and one that is full of hope and trust. The repetition of this refrain (which returns in Psalm 43 as well) is reminiscent of our inner struggles which return over and over again.

TO THINK ABOUT . . .

Do you recognise this inner conversation? How does your inner conversation go in times of trouble? Is your refrain one of hope and trust or despair and hopelessness?

'Deep calls to deep' (verse 7)

In the second half of the Psalm, the water imagery moves from refreshing streams to the pounding terror of fast-moving water. The language pulls together two powerful images – the roar of waterfalls and the crashing of the waves of the sea – and recognises their emotional power and resonance with the tumult of our inner selves.

SPACE TO DOODLE

Think about the sea or about waterfalls/wide rivers full of water. What language would you use to describe how they make you feel? Do they make you feel despairing or hopeful?

Water and the Old Testament

It is often noted that the Old Testament presents two different ideas of water which reflect its different geographical terrains: the longing for water that you get in the desert and the terror of water that comes from the fear of flooding or from a storm at sea that might shipwreck your boat.

TO THINK ABOUT . . .

Spend some time thinking about water as refreshing and water as terrifying. Which resonates with you more at the moment?

Now go back and read the Psalm again slowly. Make a note this time of the words that you notice. Are they the same or have they changed? As you finish your reflection on the Psalm, you might like to ask yourself three questions:

- How did it make me feel?
- What did it make me think about?
- What do I now need to pray for/about?

Psalm 46

Most of the Psalms we have explored so far are individual Psalms – Psalms that reflect an individual's challenges and faith in God. Psalm 46, importantly, is a community Psalm of confidence in God, an opportunity for the whole of God's people to gather together and declare their trust in God who always protects them. Although in some ways all the Psalms are community Psalms because they speak on behalf of all God's people, there are some – like this one – that make it very clear that this is not just one person speaking on behalf of everyone, but all of God's people gathering together in lament or, as here, in praise.

It is impossible to work out from the details contained in the Psalm what particular event gave rise to it, but it seems likely that this Psalm was written at a time of national emergency and crisis, at a time of threat for the nation as a whole. In response to this threat, people gathered to declare their faith in the God who is 'an ever-present help in trouble'.

The wording of this Psalm has inspired many people over the years, not least the protestant reformer Martin Luther who wrote a hymn called 'A Mighty Fortress is our God' based on this Psalm.

 Read the Psalm slowly. What words or phrases jump out at you?

Psalm 46

For the director of music. Of the Sons of Korah.
According to alamoth. *A song.*

¹ God is our refuge and strength,
    an ever-present help in trouble.
² Therefore we will not fear, though the earth give way
    and the mountains fall into the heart of the sea,
³ though its waters roar and foam
    and the mountains quake with their surging.

⁴ There is a river whose streams make glad the city
        of God,
    the holy place where the Most High dwells.
⁵ God is within her, she will not fall;
    God will help her at break of day.
⁶ Nations are in uproar, kingdoms fall;
    he lifts his voice, the earth melts.

⁷ The Lord Almighty is with us;
    the God of Jacob is our fortress.

⁸ Come and see what the Lord has done,
    the desolations he has brought on the earth.
⁹ He makes wars cease
    to the ends of the earth.
  He breaks the bow and shatters the spear;
    he burns the shields with fire.
¹⁰ He says, 'Be still, and know that I am God;
    I will be exalted among the nations,
    I will be exalted in the earth.'

¹¹ The Lord Almighty is with us;
    the God of Jacob is our fortress.

STANDING BACK
Looking at the whole Psalm

Community Psalms – whether of lament or, as here, confidence –
are fascinating. Today we rarely gather in this kind of way with
a common voice to express our sorrow or joy or trust in God –
unless, of course, you count public worship and the hymns and
songs we sing during a service, though they often focus more on
individuals than communal groups.

TO THINK ABOUT . . .

Reflect on the idea of community Psalms. Think about
the context of your family, your church or your nation. If
you were to write a Psalm together as a community, what
would it say?

The Psalm falls into three sections:

- verses 1-3: God as a shelter and refuge;

- verses 4-7: God's city and what it is like;

- verse 8-11: An invitation to see what God has done.

SPACE TO DOODLE

Pause over these three sections. How are they connected to each other?

ZOOMING IN
Picking up some details

'Refuge' (verse 1)

God is described in verse 1 as:

- 'refuge' or 'shelter': this word is most often used to describe shelter from the rain or the cold;

- 'strength': this word could also be translated as 'refuge' and means 'strong protection';

- 'help in trouble': this implies coming to the rescue when you need help.

These three words combine to give the sense of a God who takes care of us when we need it.

TO THINK ABOUT . . .

Reflect on the three words – shelter from the rain; strong protection from danger; help in times of trouble. What comes to mind when you think of them?

'Though the earth give way' (verse 2)

Verses 2-3 probably describe an earthquake and/or a tsunami. These would have been common in Israel in this period, though no less unsettling for their regularity. Throughout the Psalms, the sea is often regarded as uncontrollable and chaotic; this kind of language refers not just to tsunamis but also to the storms that would regularly occur at sea. Against the chaos of the sea, God is shown as being in full control (think also of the miracles in the Gospels in which Jesus shows himself to be more powerful than the storms at sea).

SPACE TO DOODLE The thought of a shelter/secure place when the whole world is shaking around you is vivid. Thinking about this experience, what image of unshakeability would you use?

'The city of God' (verse 4)

In a similar way to Psalm 42, the psalmist makes a great contrast between the river, whose streams rejoice in or make glad God's city, and other waters. Outside the city the sea crashes and foams, bringing chaos in its wake, but inside the city water is refreshing and joyful.

TO THINK ABOUT . . .

Look at the language of chaos used in verses 1-3 and of calm stability in verses 4-5. Jot down or sketch the images that come to mind as you observe the contrast.

QUITE INTERESTING

In verse 7, notice that another word is used of God's protection – this time the word is 'fortress'. The word actually means 'a high place'. It was hence very secure because castles on the top of hills are harder to attack than those elsewhere.

'Come and see' (verse 8)

Of course, it doesn't matter how powerful and caring God is if we don't take notice of it. The phrase 'come and see' invites us to pay attention to who God is and what God has done in the world.

TO THINK ABOUT . . .

Sit with the phrase 'come and see' for a while. What might you have missed about what God has done?

QUITE INTERESTING

'According to *alamoth*'. Like Psalm 42, this Psalm comes from the sons of Korah (see note on Psalm 42). In the Psalter, this instruction occurs only here, but the word is also used in 1 Chronicles 15:20 which refers to playing the lyres 'according to *alamoth*'. The implication is that it is a tune. Some think it refers to female voices since the word is connected to the Hebrew for 'young women', but as the 1 Chronicles usage refers to lyres (stringed instruments), it might just mean a high tune.

'He makes wars cease' (verse 9)

The obvious question asked throughout Christian history is, 'If God can make wars cease, why does he not do it more often?' There is, sadly, no easy answer to this impossible question, only more questions.

TO THINK ABOUT . . .

What would you say if someone were to ask you this?

'Be still, and know that I am God' (verse 10)

This may be one of the most quoted and sung verses from the whole of the Psalter. It is worth noting that it does *not* mean there is no need to do good in the world because God will do it. It has sometimes been interpreted in this way and, from the context, it is clear that this is a misunderstanding of this famous verse.

The Hebrew word means to sink down or relax. As a result, it seems to be suggesting that we should stop running around terrified of what is going on, worried about things in the world that we can't control, and instead rest on the knowledge of who God is.

SPACE TO DOODLE   **What does this famous verse mean to you?**

Now go back and read the Psalm again slowly. Make a note this time of the words that you notice. Are they the same or have they changed? As you finish your reflection on the Psalm, you might like to ask yourself three questions:

- How did it make me feel?

- What did it make me think about?

- What do I now need to pray for/about?

Psalm 88

Psalm 88 has the slightly unenviable honour of being the bleakest Psalm in the whole of the Psalter. Unlike most other Psalms of lament, Psalm 88 is desolate from beginning to end. Most other laments pause the despair at some point, at the beginning, in the middle or at the end, to express trust or confidence in God. This Psalm does not. What is more, the psalmist feels not only as though God has abandoned them but also that God caused the whole situation in the first place.

This Psalm reminds us that there really is nothing that we can't say to God. Although there is no response, the psalmist's railing against God feels profoundly important and something that, no matter how uncomfortable it feels to us, we should reflect on. The underlying message of this Psalm seems to be that we can say to God whatever lies on our hearts. Nothing is out of bounds. The key thing is not what we say but that we keep on speaking to him, even in the worst of times.

 Read the Psalm slowly. What words or phrases jump out at you?

Psalm 88

A song. A psalm of the Sons of Korah. For the director of music. According to mahalath leannoth. *A maskil of Heman the Ezrahite.*

¹ LORD, you are the God who saves me;
     day and night I cry out to you.
² May my prayer come before you;
     turn your ear to my cry.

³ I am overwhelmed with troubles
     and my life draws near to death.
⁴ I am counted among those who go down to the pit;
     I am like one without strength.
⁵ I am set apart with the dead,
     like the slain who lie in the grave,
   whom you remember no more,
     who are cut off from your care.

⁶ You have put me in the lowest pit,
     in the darkest depths.
⁷ Your wrath lies heavily on me;
     you have overwhelmed me with all your waves.
⁸ You have taken from me my closest friends
     and have made me repulsive to them.
   I am confined and cannot escape;
⁹ my eyes are dim with grief.
   I call to you, LORD, every day;
     I spread out my hands to you.
¹⁰ Do you show your wonders to the dead?
     Do their spirits rise up and praise you?
¹¹ Is your love declared in the grave,
     your faithfulness in Destruction?

¹² Are your wonders known in the place of darkness,
    or your righteous deeds in the land of oblivion?

¹³ But I cry to you for help, LORD;
    in the morning my prayer comes before you.
¹⁴ Why, LORD, do you reject me
    and hide your face from me?

¹⁵ From my youth I have suffered and been close
        to death;
    I have borne your terrors and am in despair.
¹⁶ Your wrath has swept over me;
    your terrors have destroyed me.
¹⁷ All day long they surround me like a flood;
    they have completely engulfed me.
¹⁸ You have taken from me friend and neighbour –
    darkness is my closest friend.

STANDING BACK
Looking at the whole Psalm

'I cry out to you'

Psalm 88 is organised around the words cry/call in verses 1-2, 9 and 13. The repetition of calling out to God is powerful as we read through the Psalm. There is a wonderful parable in Luke's Gospel (18:1-8) which features a widow who pesters and pesters a judge until he gives in. This Psalm feels a little like that. The psalmist keeps on calling to God and never stops.

TO THINK ABOUT . . .

Think about the repetition of the words cry/call. Why do you think the psalmist does this?

'I am overwhelmed with troubles'

Notice that verses 3-9 and 15-18 mirror each other in containing the psalmist's agony. It is striking that he returns to the same themes again in the second half of the Psalm.

SPACE TO DOODLE

Jot down the different words that the psalmist uses to describe the misery he experiences. Or even sketch what it feels like to be overwhelmed with troubles.

ZOOMING IN
Picking up some details

The title: 'According to *mahalath leannoth*. A *maskil* of Heman the Ezrahite'

Psalm 88 has one of the longest titles in the Psalms. It is declared to be:

- a song;

- a Psalm which, like Psalms 42 and 46, is Korahite or 'of the Sons of Korah' (see Psalm 42 for more on them);

- for the director of music;

- 'according to *mahalath leannoth*.' No one knows what this means, but it probably refers to a tune that we no longer have access to;

- a *maskil*. Like Psalm 42, this Psalm seems to be a Psalm of contemplation or pondering;

- of Heman the Ezrahite. In addition to being associated with the Sons of Korah, this Psalm has a named author. If this Heman is the same as the Heman mentioned in 1 Kings and 1 Chronicles, then he was a musician (1 Chr. 6:33), a Levite and a Kohathite (which may well be the same as a Korahite). He may also be the Heman who was set aside as a prophet (1 Chr. 25:1) and who had a reputation for wisdom (1 Kgs 4:31).

TO THINK ABOUT . . .

If this is a *maskil*, or Psalm of contemplation, what would you say is the main focus of the psalmist's pondering?

'You are the God who saves me' (verse 1)

One of the striking contrasts in the Psalm is between this opening line and the rest of the Psalm. It is the closest the psalmist gets to a statement of confidence in God. The challenge it throws up is that the psalmist appears to have long-term problems yet still feels able to declare that God is a 'God who saves me'.

TO THINK ABOUT . . .

Reflect on the phrase, 'You are the God who saves me'. What do you think it means here, when God clearly hasn't – yet – done anything to save the psalmist from his troubles?

'I am counted among those who go down to the pit' (verse 4)

The psalmist's language here might be translated in modern idiom as, 'I am as good as dead.' He feels as though his life is over – it is not clear whether he is talking about a physical or an emotional state, and it doesn't really matter. The effect is the same whichever he means.

TO THINK ABOUT . . .

Here and in verses 15-16 the psalmist is clinging on by his fingertips. Spend some time in prayer, holding before God all those who feel like this today (and if it's you, hold yourself there too).

'You have taken me from my closest friends' (verse 8)

It is fascinating to notice that, in the midst of despair, what the psalmist's feels keenly is the loss of friends (see verse 8 and 18). On top of everything else, he feels lost and alone.

TO THINK ABOUT . . .

Think about the effect of loneliness in this Psalm and in the world around you. Pray for those who feel lonely today. Use the space here to jot down the names of those you know of who are in particular need of prayer today.

'Do you show your wonders to the dead?' (verses 10-12)

Verses 10-12 contain six rhetorical questions – all addressed to God – the answer to each, if any were needed, would clearly be no.

SPACE TO DOODLE

Reflect on this string of questions. If you are feeling like the psalmist does in Psalm 88, what questions are you asking God right now?

QUITE INTERESTING

The word translated 'death' in verse 3 is the Hebrew word *sheol*. Throughout the Old Testament, *sheol* is used for the place to which the dead go when they die. It is described as though it is an actual place below the earth. It is nothing like our popular idea of 'hell' as the devil is not there, there is no fire nor any kind of punishment. The dead exist (and interestingly are still within God's reach), but nothing more happens to them. In this sense, 'death' is a good translation of the word. The next verse, verse 4, contains a parallel idea – the psalmist is counted as someone who has already gone down to the pit/*sheol*.

'Darkness is my closest friend' (verse 18)

As we noted in the introduction, this Psalm ends as it begins – in utter darkness.

TO THINK ABOUT . . .

What effect does the ending have on you? Do you find it powerful or a bit disappointing?

Now go back and read the Psalm again slowly. Make a note this time of the words that you notice. Are they the same or have they changed? As you finish your reflection on the Psalm, you might like to ask yourself three questions:

- How did it make me feel?
- What did it make me think about?
- What do I now need to pray for/about?

....
....
....
....
....
....
....
....
....
....
....
....
....
....
....
....
....
....
....
....
....

Psalm 104

Psalm 104 is one of a number of creation Psalms. One of the key themes of this kind of Psalm is the way in which creation, in all its glory and splendour, turns the heart towards the creator in wonder and praise. There is something powerful about pausing and reminding ourselves of the awesome wonder of creation and allowing ourselves to praise the God who brought it all into being. The twentieth-century hymn, 'O Lord my God, when I in awesome wonder', mimics the movements and praise of these creation Psalms. As you prepare yourself to reflect on this Psalm, you might like to sing or listen to that hymn.

You may also like to look at the previous Psalm, Psalm 103. Whereas Psalm 104 celebrates God's greatness as creator, 103 celebrates God's goodness and care for all God's people. They are often regarded as twin Psalms to be read together.

 Read the Psalm slowly. What words or phrases jump out at you?

Psalm 104

¹ Praise the LORD, my soul.

LORD my God, you are very great;
you are clothed with splendour and majesty.

² The LORD wraps himself in light as with a garment;
he stretches out the heavens like a tent
and lays the beams of his upper chambers on their
waters.
³ He makes the clouds his chariot
and rides on the wings of the wind.
⁴ He makes winds his messengers,
flames of fire his servants.

⁵ He set the earth on its foundations;
it can never be moved.
⁶ You covered it with the watery depths as with a garment;
the waters stood above the mountains.
⁷ But at your rebuke the waters fled,
at the sound of your thunder they took to flight;
⁸ they flowed over the mountains,
they went down into the valleys,
to the place you assigned for them.
⁹ You set a boundary they cannot cross;
never again will they cover the earth.

¹⁰ He makes springs pour water into the ravines;
it flows between the mountains.
¹¹ They give water to all the beasts of the field;
the wild donkeys quench their thirst.
¹² The birds of the sky nest by the waters;
they sing among the branches.
¹³ He waters the mountains from his upper chambers;
the land is satisfied by the fruit of his work.

¹⁴ He makes grass grow for the cattle,
    and plants for people to cultivate –
    bringing forth food from the earth:
¹⁵ wine that gladdens human hearts,
    oil to make their faces shine,
    and bread that sustains their hearts.
¹⁶ The trees of the LORD are well watered,
    the cedars of Lebanon that he planted.
¹⁷ There the birds make their nests;
    the stork has its home in the junipers.
¹⁸ The high mountains belong to the wild goats;
    the crags are a refuge for the hyrax.

¹⁹ He made the moon to mark the seasons,
    and the sun knows when to go down.
²⁰ You bring darkness, it becomes night,
    and all the beasts of the forest prowl.
²¹ The lions roar for their prey
    and seek their food from God.
²² The sun rises, and they steal away;
    they return and lie down in their dens.
²³ Then people go out to their work,
    to their labour until evening.

²⁴ How many are your works, LORD!
    In wisdom you made them all;
    the earth is full of your creatures.
²⁵ There is the sea, vast and spacious,
    teeming with creatures beyond number –
    living things both large and small.
²⁶ There the ships go to and fro,
    and Leviathan, which you formed to frolic there.
²⁷ All creatures look to you
    to give them their food at the proper time.

[28] When you give it to them,
    they gather it up;
  when you open your hand,
    they are satisfied with good things.
[29] When you hide your face,
    they are terrified;
  when you take away their breath,
    they die and return to the dust.
[30] When you send your Spirit,
    they are created,
    and you renew the face of the ground.

[31] May the glory of the LORD endure forever;
    may the LORD rejoice in his works –
[32] he who looks at the earth, and it trembles,
    who touches the mountains, and they smoke.

[33] I will sing to the LORD all my life;
    I will sing praise to my God as long as I live.
[34] May my meditation be pleasing to him,
    as I rejoice in the LORD.
[35] But may sinners vanish from the earth
    and the wicked be no more.

Praise the LORD, my soul.

Praise the LORD.

STANDING BACK
Looking at the whole Psalm

'You are very great'

The structure of Psalm 104 is interesting.

The first line of verse 1 summons the 'soul' to praise God; the second half of verse 1 turns to address God ('you are very great; you are clothed with splendour and majesty'). The next 22 verses (up to the end of verse 23) enumerate God's acts as creator, and then the psalmist returns in verse 24 to address God directly again ('How many are your works, Lord!').

Within these 22 verses:

- verses 2-9 set out the basic structure of the created world (note that the psalmist, in common with the other biblical writers, imagines the earth surrounded by water, set on pillars with the water above held back by a firmament);

- verses 10-18 focus on water and its role in so many parts of creation;

- verses 19-23 explore time, both day and night.

All the themes laid out in these first 23 verses are macro themes – broad brush strokes of creation.

Verse 24 shifts attention from the macro to the micro. After praising God again, the psalmist turns for a brief moment to God's 'creatures', those who live in the sea (verse 25) or sail on it (verse 26).

TO THINK ABOUT . . .

Trace the focus of the Psalm from verse 2 to verse 26.
What sense of God and God's role in creation do you get
from these passages?

The shorter later section of the Psalm (verses 27-32) speaks of the utter dependency of God's creatures upon their creator both positively and negatively, before the psalmist ends by extending his personal praises to God once more (verses 33-5).

TO THINK ABOUT . . .

Reflect on verses 27-32 and the strong sense of dependency on God to bring life and to take it away again. How to you respond to this idea that everything is completely in the hands of God?

ZOOMING IN
Picking up some details

'In light as with a garment' (verse 2)

The first section of the Psalm (verses 2-9) uses strong metaphors to describe God's act of creation, employing the imagery of garments and tents, chariots and wings. Strikingly, the language suggests that creation both reveals who God is and conceals him.

Probably most importantly of all, it uses everyday examples – getting dressed and erecting tents – to describe the great mystery of creation. If I had been writing this Psalm, I might have chosen more elaborate or majestic illustrations. There is something evocative, however, in recognising that for God, creating the world was as easy as putting up a tent.

SPACE TO DOODLE — **What image from this Psalm most captures your imagination? Jot it down or sketch it here.**

'Set a boundary' (verse 9)

The theme of God bringing order out of chaos runs through many of the Psalms. Here in the long first section of Psalm 104, it takes the form of placing and shaping the world as well as time periods to govern day and night.

TO THINK ABOUT . . .

Reflect on the importance of boundaries for bringing order and life out of chaos. Where are the boundaries in your life that most bring you life? Are there any parts of your life where you need more boundaries?

QUITE INTERESTING

This Psalm is of one of thirty-four Psalms that have no title: 1, 2, 10, 33, 43, 71, 91, 93–7, 99, 104–7, 111–19, 135–7, 146–50). It isn't entirely clear why these have been preserved without a title, but it does mean that they have no tune or style ascribed to them.

'Quench their thirst' (verse 11)

Throughout the whole of the Old Testament, water is both a dangerous chaos that needs taming and a source of life and nourishment. This Psalm, possibly more clearly than anywhere else, makes clear the connection between these two apparently contradictory statements. The waters of the deep are dangerous and terrifying, but when God tames them, as he did in creation and has continued to do ever since, they become life-giving and nourishing. It is the act of God that turns something fearful into something safe and good.

TO THINK ABOUT ...

Reflect on verses 10-18 and the language used of God bringing life through water. Have you ever experienced God transforming something terrifying into something life-giving?

'How many are your works' (verse 24)

The repetition of the number and variety of God's creation is built up over a few verses.

Verses 24-7 celebrate the variety of God's creation:

- God's works are 'many' (verse 24);

- 'the earth is full of your creatures' (verse 24);

- the vast and spacious sea teems with creatures (verse 25);

- all creatures depend on him (verse 27).

TO THINK ABOUT . . .

Why is variety so important to the psalmist, do you think? What does this tell us about God as creator?

'Take away their breath . . . send your Spirit' (verses 29-30)

It is impossible to translate into English, but the Hebrew word for breath and for Spirit is the same (*ruaḥ*) so the end of verse 29 and beginning of verse 30 are a play on words. When God takes away the breath/Spirit, people die; when God sends breath/Spirit, new life is created and the earth is renewed.

TO THINK ABOUT . . .

Think about the story of Pentecost, when a wind blew from heaven and filled all the disciples with the Holy Spirit (Acts 2:1-2). In what ways do you find the depiction of the Holy Spirit as wind or breath helpful?

'May the LORD rejoice in his works' (verse 31)

The Psalm ends as it began, with praise of God. This particular phrase stands out, however. God created the world in order to delight in it. Here the psalmist prays that God would be able to continue delighting in the world that he has made. The God whose power can make mountains tremble is also the God who gains delight from his creation.

SPACE TO DOODLE

God's creation includes you. What do you think most delights God about you?

Now go back and read the Psalm again slowly. Make a note this time of the words that you notice. Are they the same or have they changed? As you finish your reflection on the Psalm, you might like to ask yourself three questions:

- How did it make me feel?

- What did it make me think about?

- What do I now need to pray for/about?

....
....
....
....
....
....
....
....
....
....
....
....
....
....
....
....
....
....
....
....
....
....

Psalm 118

....

Psalm 118 is the last in a collection of Psalms (111–18)
known as the *hallel* or hallelujah Psalms because they focus on
praise (*hallel*). Psalm 118 records the experience of an unknown
king who went out to fight a battle and almost lost but, at the
last moment, was saved by God and has now returned to the
temple to praise God for his help.

The Psalm contains a number of verses that are important
within the Gospels, and hence within the Christian tradition.
It is also significant within Jewish tradition. After the time
of the New Testament, Psalm 118 was recited during the
Passover meal, with Psalms 113 and 114 before the meal and
Psalms 115–18 recited at its conclusion. Jewish tradition also
associates Psalm 118 with the Feast of Tabernacles, especially
the procession around the altar which took place on seven
successive days. Although these traditions emerged after the
time of Jesus, there is plenty of evidence that Psalm 118 was well
known and well loved during the New Testament period.

 **Read the Psalm slowly. What words or phrases jump
out at you?**

Psalm 118

¹ Give thanks to the LORD, for he is good;
   his love endures forever.

² Let Israel say:
   'His love endures forever.'
³ Let the house of Aaron say:
   'His love endures forever.'
⁴ Let those who fear the LORD say:
   'His love endures forever.'

⁵ When hard pressed, I cried to the LORD;
   he brought me into a spacious place.
⁶ The LORD is with me; I will not be afraid.
   What can mere mortals do to me?
⁷ The LORD is with me; he is my helper.
   I look in triumph on my enemies.

⁸ It is better to take refuge in the LORD
   than to trust in humans.
⁹ It is better to take refuge in the LORD
   than to trust in princes.
¹⁰ All the nations surrounded me,
   but in the name of the LORD I cut them down.
¹¹ They surrounded me on every side,
   but in the name of the LORD I cut them down.
¹² They swarmed around me like bees,
   but they were consumed as quickly as burning thorns;
   in the name of the LORD I cut them down.
¹³ I was pushed back and about to fall,
   but the LORD helped me.
¹⁴ The LORD is my strength and my defence;
   he has become my salvation.

¹⁵ Shouts of joy and victory
    resound in the tents of the righteous:
  'The LORD's right hand has done mighty things!
¹⁶ The LORD's right hand is lifted high;
    the LORD's right hand has done mighty things!'
¹⁷ I will not die but live,
    and will proclaim what the LORD has done.
¹⁸ The LORD has chastened me severely,
    but he has not given me over to death.
¹⁹ Open for me the gates of the righteous;
    I will enter and give thanks to the LORD.
²⁰ This is the gate of the LORD
    through which the righteous may enter.
²¹ I will give you thanks, for you answered me;
    you have become my salvation.

²² The stone the builders rejected
    has become the cornerstone;
²³ the LORD has done this,
    and it is marvellous in our eyes.
²⁴ The LORD has done it this very day;
    let us rejoice today and be glad.

²⁵ LORD, save us!
    LORD, grant us success!

²⁶ Blessed is he who comes in the name of the LORD.
    From the house of the LORD we bless you.
²⁷ The LORD is God,
    and he has made his light shine on us.
  With boughs in hand, join in the festal procession
    up to the horns of the altar.

²⁸ You are my God, and I will praise you;
    you are my God, and I will exalt you.

²⁹ Give thanks to the LORD, for he is good;
    his love endures forever.

STANDING BACK
Looking at the whole Psalm

Many voices, one Psalm

Scholars agree that it is likely that we can hear in this Psalm the voices of different people involved in worship.

- Verses 1-4 are a call to worship, possibly by the priests in the temple.

- Verses 5-19 focus on the words of someone – probably a king – who was coming to the temple to give thanks for his victory in battle.

- Verses 20-8 feature a number of voices – the king, the priests and the crowd – who all give thanks for the victory.

- Verse 29 ends the Psalm as it began.

TO THINK ABOUT . . .

Spend some time looking at the different sections of the Psalm and seeing if you can 'hear' the different voices speaking. Pay particular attention to verses 20-8 where the voices are more mixed. Are there any 'voices' in the Psalm that you relate to more than others?

Psalm 118 was important in the early church – we can tell this by how often it was cited in the New Testament.

TO THINK ABOUT . . .

Go through the Psalm and pick out the verses you recognise. If you find yourself unsure and want to check, these verses from the New Testament all refer back to Psalm 118: Hebrews 13:6; Matthew 21:9, 42; 1 Peter 2:4, 7. Why do you think that this Psalm was so well loved by New Testament writers?

ZOOMING IN
Picking up some details

'Give thanks to the LORD, for he is good' (verse 1)

The opening verse of the Psalm is common within the Old Testament (see Pss. 106:1; 107:1; 136:1; 1 Chr. 16:34; 2 Chr. 5:13; 7:3; 20:21) and invites worshippers to call to mind and give thanks for God's goodness.

Notice how different groups are identified and invited to join in – Israel (i.e. God's people), the house of Aaron (i.e. the priests) and those who fear the Lord. It is not entirely clear whether this final group is a summary of the previous two groups (Israel and the house of Aaron) or a new group of people who were Gentiles but worshipped God. Either option would work here.

Whoever they were, they were all invited to give thanks for God's *hesed*. This word is one of the most important in all of the Old Testament and refers to God's steadfast, unwavering love. It can also be translated as loving kindness.

TO THINK ABOUT . . .

Read through the Psalm and circle all the times the word
'love' is used.

If you were asked to give an example of God's steadfast,
unwavering love in your life, what example would you
give?

'When hard pressed . . . spacious place' (verse 5)

The Hebrew of verse 5 features a play on words that the NIV tries to reflect. Notice the contrast between 'hard pressed' and 'spacious place'; another way of putting this is would be in 'narrow straits' and then a 'broad place'.

TO THINK ABOUT . . .

Think of a time or place in which you have felt 'hard pressed'.

Then think of a time or place in which you have felt you were in a 'spacious place'.

What words would you choose to describe the difference between both experiences?

'The LORD is my strength' (verse 14)

The psalmist reflects here on what God has done for him with three words:

- strength: the word refers to the idea of might, boldness or sheer physical strength;

- defence: this word can either be translated as 'might' and therefore be quite close to strength, or it can be translated as 'song' and hence have an entirely different meaning;

- salvation: this is the same word as we might use for salvation generally. In this instance it is used literally: God has saved him from disaster.

SPACE TO DOODLE

Think about verse 14. Reflect on the psalmist's language for God: strength, defence (or song!) and salvation. 'The Lord is my _____ and my _____. He has become my _____.' What words would you put in the blanks?

QUITE INTERESTING

Psalm 118 – like the rest of the *hallel* Psalms – has no title and hence no tune or style ascribed to it. This is particularly interesting given the kingly focus of the Psalm, which might suggest a connection with David.

'The stone the builders rejected' (verse 22)

The image of the stone used here (and picked up in the New Testament and used of Jesus, see Matthew 21:42) is a vivid one. Stones used for buildings were 'dressed' before use. This means that they were cut to size. Builders, who by and large did not use mortar, would select stones to fit with the other stones so there would be a good strong structure. Stones that did not fit with the others were discarded. A cornerstone was the base stone at the corner to which the other stones would then be fitted. In other words, this Psalm is saying that the stone that didn't fit with the rest and so was thrown away has become the stone to which all the other stones in the building must now be fitted.

SPACE TO DOODLE

Reflect on this image. What do you think it means in this Psalm? And what do you think it means when applied to Jesus in the New Testament?

How might you depict Jesus the cornerstone?

Hosanna (verse 26)

The word 'hosanna' has become very important in Christian worship, but it occurs only in the Gospel accounts of Jesus' entry into Jerusalem' when the crowd shouted:

> 'Hosanna to the Son of David!'
> 'Blessed is he who comes in the name of the Lord!'
> 'Hosanna in the highest heaven!'
> (Matt. 21:9)

This is a version – albeit changed – of Psalm 118:25-6. The Hebrew words for 'save us' (verse 25) are *hoshea na* which mean literally, 'Save now!' If you take those Hebrew letters and put them into Greek letters (without translating at all), then you get 'hosanna'.

TO THINK ABOUT . . .

The original Hebrew words meant 'save us', but the New Testament Greek transliteration appears to be used as a shout of triumph. Reflect on the difference. How do you think this movement from plea for help to celebration happened?

Now go back and read the Psalm again slowly. Make a note this time of the words that you notice. Are they the same or have they changed? As you finish your reflection on the Psalm, you might like to ask yourself three questions:

- How did it make me feel?
- What did it make me think about?
- What do I now need to pray for/about?

....

....

....

....

....

....

....

....

....

....

....

....

....

....

....

....

....

....

....

Psalm 121

Psalm 121 rivals Psalm 23 for popularity. This is because, like Psalm 23, it provides a message of reassurance that throughout all the dangers of life God takes care of us and guards us. The Psalm moves from the very personal ('he will not let your foot slip') to the national ('he who watches over Israel') and back again, reminding us that all aspects of life, from the personal to the universal, are in the care of God.

The title of Psalm 121 informs us that, in common with fourteen other Psalms (Psalms 120–34), it was 'a song of ascents' – in other words, a song sung by pilgrims on their way up to Jerusalem to celebrate one of the three major festivals: Passover, Pentecost and Tabernacles. Today, the first verse of the Psalm is particularly beloved by those who enjoy hill or fell walking and those who enjoy travelling in general. David Livingstone is said to have read this Psalm with this family before setting sail for Africa. Also important is verse 2, 'the Maker of heaven and earth', which is quoted verbatim in the Apostles' Creed.

 Read the Psalm slowly. What words or phrases jump out at you?

Psalm 121

A song of ascents.

¹ I lift up my eyes to the mountains –
  where does my help come from?
² My help comes from the LORD,
  the Maker of heaven and earth.

³ He will not let your foot slip –
  he who watches over you will not slumber;
⁴ indeed, he who watches over Israel
  will neither slumber nor sleep.

⁵ The LORD watches over you –
  the LORD is your shade at your right hand;
⁶ the sun will not harm you by day,
  nor the moon by night.

⁷ The LORD will keep you from all harm –
  he will watch over your life;
⁸ the LORD will watch over your coming and going
  both now and for evermore.

STANDING BACK
Looking at the whole Psalm

Similar to Psalm 118, scholars think that it is possible to hear different voices speaking in this Psalm, though this time there are only two. The first two verses may represent the voice of a pilgrim who, in looking around, is fearful of the danger that might befall him and reminds himself of the care of God as he travels along. The last six verses may be a pronouncement of reassurance from a second person who reminds the pilgrim that God will take care of him.

TO THINK ABOUT . . .

Reflect on the change of tone between verses 1-2 and 3-8. In what kind of context do you think they might have been said?

Psalms 120–34 all have the same title: 'A song of ascents'. Many of them refer regularly to Jerusalem or Zion, which is on a hill, hence the idea that you 'go up' to Jerusalem. Some think this means that these fifteen Psalms were set to be sung on the way to the temple and that they were imported into the Psalter as an entire collection.

SPACE
TO
DOODLE

If you have time, read all fifteen songs of ascent (Psalms 120–34); if not, read just this one. Either way, reflect on the themes of pilgrimage you find.

ZOOMING IN
Picking up some details

'I lift up my eyes to the mountains' (verse 1)

The King James Bible translation of this verse famously renders it as:

> I will lift up mine eyes unto the hills, from whence cometh my help.

The implication of this is that God lives in the hills and therefore provides help from there. Most modern scholars would point out that it is much more likely that this was a question ('Where does my help come from?') rather than a statement.

Nevertheless, there remain two different ways to understand this opening verse:

- The mountains/hills are frightening to the psalmist on the way to Jerusalem as the place where wild beasts or bandits might lie in wait. In this case, the psalmist would lift up his eyes in hope that God would send help.

- The mountains/hills refer to Mount Zion as the place where God dwells. From them, the psalmist hopes help will come (hence much closer to the KJV translation).

In essence, the question is whether hills suggest danger or assurance of strength and help. It is, of course, possible that the psalmist might have feared the hills, whereas we might find strength in them.

SPACE
TO
DOODLE

Think about the hills or mountains that you know. Do you see them as places of danger or of reassurance? Does this feature in your prayers at all?

'Maker of heaven and earth' (verse 2)

The psalmist reassures himself that help always comes from God, the God who made the entirety of the world – both heaven and earth – from the highest point of the sky to the lowest depths of the earth. As a result, God can more than match any danger the pilgrim might encounter on the way to Jerusalem.

TO THINK ABOUT . . .

Reflect on the connection between God as creator and God as helper – i.e. the God who will come to our aid when we need it. In what way do you find this reassuring?

He 'will not slumber' (verses 3-4)

Verses 3-4 unpack what it means to the pilgrim that God will provide help:

- He will not let the pilgrim's foot slip or stumble.

- God will never slumber or sleep.

In other words, God will ensure not only that the pilgrim travels safely but also that he will be attentive every hour of every day.

QUITE INTERESTING

The word for 'slumber' also means to be drowsy. The image is of someone on a hot summer's day sitting down and getting drowsy as they wait for something to happen. God is not like this. His loving attention will never waver.

TO THINK ABOUT . . .

How do you react to the statement of God's constant attentiveness, never sleeping for a moment?

'The LORD' (verse 5-8)

In verses 3-4, God is referred to by a pronoun, but in verses 5-8 he is named – *YHWH*, the Lord. It is this change which suggests that a different person is now speaking, one who reassures the pilgrim with statements about God's nature and, therefore, what he will do.

There is a word that is repeated three times in these verses and translated here as keeper/keep. The word (*shomer)* means 'to guard, keep safe or watch over'.

TO THINK ABOUT . . .

Reflect on the impact of the repetition of name of God ('the LORD') and of the word 'keep' or 'guard'. What effect does this have on you?

'Your coming and going' (verse 8)

The final verse acts as a benediction for all kinds of travel: the God who helps, who makes sure your foot does not slip and who never sleeps, will watch over every journey you take (going out and coming back) – literally 'from now until eternity'.

TO THINK ABOUT . . .

The wording at the end of this Psalm is beautiful – you might like to try and reword it as a modern-day blessing on those who travel.

Now go back and read the Psalm again slowly. Make a note this time of the words that you notice. Are they the same or have they changed? As you finish your reflection on the Psalm, you might like to ask yourself three questions:

- How did it make me feel?

- What did it make me think about?

- What do I now need to pray for/about?

....
....
....
....
....
....
....
....
....
....
....
....
....
....
....
....
....
....
....

Psalm 130

Psalm 130, often known as *De Profundis* from its first
two words in Latin, reflects a heartfelt cry to God from the
midst of a crisis. Historically, this Psalm has often been used at
funerals because of the grief and disorientation it displays. Some
argue that it should be read with the previous Psalm, Psalm
129, which talks extensively about the ways that the faithful
are persecuted by those around them. That Psalm could seem
slightly self-righteous and arrogant if read on its own, but if
paired with this Psalm, a Psalm that acknowledges the sinfulness
of the psalmist, a balance is brought to them both. One of the
key features of this Psalm is the psalmist's utter dependence on
God for mercy and help when he needs it most.

There is something particularly evocative about the Psalm's
opening phrase. Even though it might not be a phrase we would
normally use today, 'out of the depths' beautifully captures the
sense that sometimes we are in the depths of despair and our
only option is to cry to God from there.

 **Read the Psalm slowly. What words or phrases jump
out at you?**

Psalm 130

A song of ascents.

¹ Out of the depths I cry to you, LORD;
²   Lord, hear my voice.
  Let your ears be attentive
    to my cry for mercy.

³ If you, LORD, kept a record of sins,
    Lord, who could stand?
⁴ But with you there is forgiveness,
    so that we can, with reverence, serve you.

⁵ I wait for the LORD, my whole being waits,
    and in his word I put my hope.
⁶ I wait for the Lord
    more than watchmen wait for the morning,
    more than watchmen wait for the morning.

⁷ Israel, put your hope in the LORD,
    for with the LORD is unfailing love
    and with him is full redemption.
⁸ He himself will redeem Israel
    from all their sins.

STANDING BACK
Looking at the whole Psalm

The dynamic of this Psalm is striking. The psalmist uses his own experience of crying out to God and waiting for God to act as an example that encourages Israel to do the same.

- Verses 1-2 consist of a plea to God for help.
- Verses 3-4 acknowledge human sinfulness but at the same time state confidence in God's forgiveness.
- Verses 5-6 stress that because of this forgiveness, the psalmist simply needs to wait for God to act.
- Verses 7-8 turn outwards to the whole of Israel and urge them to do the same.

QUITE INTERESTING

In Hebrew, the name for God, *YHWH*, is never pronounced. Instead, whenever the reader saw these four letters (sometimes known as the tetragrammaton), they would say 'Lord'. What is sometimes confusing is that in the Old Testament God is often addressed with the usual word for Lord as well (*adonai*). You can, however, tell in your English translations when 'Lord' is translated from *YHWH* and when it is translated from *adonai* because of the capitalisation of the letters. *YHWH* is written 'LORD'; *adonai* is written 'Lord'.

TO THINK ABOUT . . .

Reflect on the four sections of this Psalm. What do you notice about the movement from one couplet to the next? How do verses 7-8 relate to the rest of the Psalm?

If you were to use an example from your own life to encourage someone to trust in God, what would you choose?

YHWH - Lord

Psalm 130 uses both Lord and Lord regularly throughout, normally with 'Lord' first and 'Lord' second (the exception to this is verses 7-8, which do not include 'Lord').

TO THINK ABOUT . . .

Look carefully at Psalm 130 and notice where the psalmist has used 'Lord' or 'Lord'. The former translates *YHWH* and is God's name, and the latter *adonai*, the usual word for 'Lord'. Once you've noticed a pattern, do you have any thoughts on why it has been done like this?

ZOOMING IN
Picking up some details

The title

Notice that this Psalm, like 121, has the title of 'A song of ascents' (see note on Psalm 121 for more on what this means).

TO THINK ABOUT . . .

Think about this Psalm as one that might be said on the way to worship God in the temple in Jerusalem. How might it prepare you for worship?

'Out of the depths' (verse 1)

The word 'depths' is normally used for the sea (see for example Isa. 51:10; Ps. 69:2) and, in particular, for chaos. The sea was regarded as that place that could not be contained or controlled – except by God. As a result, it is a particularly good metaphor for those times in life when events feel as though they will overwhelm you.

SPACE TO DOODLE

Think about the sea. It can be both beautiful and terrifying, serene and chaotic. What does calling to God out of the depths conjure up for you?

'Kept a record ... forgiveness' (verses 3-4)

Forgiveness is about 'letting go' and not holding on to the sins committed. Here, the psalmist reflects on the difference between God guarding or keeping a record of sins and forgiving them. It is a strikingly vivid image, especially when coupled with the question, 'Who could stand?' The idea is that if God were to keep hold of all our sins rather than letting them go, everyone would be crushed under the burden of them.

SPACE TO DOODLE

Reflect on the emotional impact of the image here – the crushing weight of sin in contrast to the freedom that comes when God forgives. Do you relate to the imagery here?

'I wait for the LORD' (verses 5-6)

The word 'wait' is key to understanding this part of the Psalm. This is no passive waiting, ticking off the hours in the vain hope that it (whatever 'it' is) might come. This is active, edge-of-the-seat waiting with the eyes fixed on the far horizon, waiting with every fibre of your being for what you know will surely come.

To make sure we understand the image, the psalmist refers to the role of a watcher or sentinel. Their role was to scan the far horizon, constantly alert to ensure they were ready for whatever might be coming. The repetition of 'more than watchmen wait for the morning' emphasises that this is how the psalmist is waiting for God, so confident is he that God will come.

TO THINK ABOUT . . .

When was the last time you waited for something with the whole of your being? For the phone to ring? A letter to arrive? Do you wait for God with this level of anticipation?

'Unfailing love' (verses 7-8)

The Psalm ends with a recommendation to Israel that they should hope for God in the same way, because with him is unwavering love and redemption from all sin. One of the striking features of this Psalm is that there is no hint that anything external has changed. What has changed is the attitude of the psalmist – an attitude he commends to the rest of Israel.

TO THINK ABOUT . . .

Is this possible for us? To change our attitude from the despair seen in verses 1-2 to the confidence of verses 7-8? What would we need to be able to do this?

Now go back and read the Psalm again slowly. Make a note this time of the words that you notice. Are they the same or have they changed? As you finish your reflection on the Psalm, you might like to ask yourself three questions:

- How did it make me feel?
- What did it make me think about?
- What do I now need to pray for/about?

Psalm 137

Psalm 137 is a memorable Psalm, not just because of its tragic opening and horrifying ending, but because it has been set to music many times, from William Walton's 'Belshazzar's Feast' to Boney M.'s cover of 'Rivers of Babylon'. The fury demonstrated at the end stands out starkly when read alongside the previous two Psalms, 135 and 136. These two thanksgiving Psalms praise God for his goodness and for his role in creation. The switch of mood in Psalm 137 is startling.

The final verse of the Psalm has provoked extensive discussion about whether, in the context of worship, certain verses, such as this one, should be used or not. Various collections of Psalms bracket out these kinds of verses as an indication that they don't have to be used if it is felt inappropriate in the setting. Some feel very strongly that they should be left out; others equally strongly that they should be included.

 Read the Psalm slowly. What words or phrases jump out at you?

Psalm 137

¹ By the rivers of Babylon we sat and wept
    when we remembered Zion.
² There on the poplars
    we hung our harps,
³ for there our captors asked us for songs,
    our tormentors demanded songs of joy;
    they said, 'Sing us one of the songs of Zion!'

⁴ How can we sing the songs of the LORD
    while in a foreign land?
⁵ If I forget you, Jerusalem,
    may my right hand forget its skill.
⁶ May my tongue cling to the roof of my mouth
    if I do not remember you,
  if I do not consider Jerusalem
    my highest joy.

⁷ Remember, LORD, what the Edomites did
    on the day Jerusalem fell.
 'Tear it down,' they cried,
   'tear it down to its foundations!'
⁸ Daughter Babylon, doomed to destruction,
    happy is the one who repays you
    according to what you have done to us.
⁹ Happy is the one who seizes your infants
    and dashes them against the rocks.

STANDING BACK
Looking at the whole Psalm

Psalm 137 is often classed as a community lament (i.e. a lament of a group not an individual). What is odd about it, however, is that most community laments have a fixed structure, but this Psalm is different. In this regard it is unlike every other Psalm in the Psalter.

TO THINK ABOUT . . .

Look at the three different sections of the Psalm (verses 1-3; 4-6; 7-9). If you were to give each a label, what would it be?

Psalm 137 seems to be set during – or seems to be recalling – the Israelites' exile to Babylon. In 597 BC the Kingdom of Judah was besieged and defeated by the Babylonian army under the command of King Nebuchadnezzar. In punishment for their rebellion, various sections of society – including the king – were sent into exile in Babylon in three waves, in 597, 586 and 582 BC. This Psalm remembers the trauma of that experience and what it meant for their worship.

> **TO THINK ABOUT . . .**
>
> Psalm 137 recalls a national trauma and was probably sung by the Israelites together as a community. What kinds of traumas might we recall and grieve together? How might we do this in worship?

ZOOMING IN
Picking up some details

The title

This is another one of those Psalms that has no title in the original text.

> **TO THINK ABOUT . . .**
>
> If you were to give this Psalm a title, what would it be and why?

QUITE INTERESTING

The psalmist lists two enemies in this Psalm: Babylon and Edom. Babylon was the country that took them off into exile, but Edom were their near neighbours to the southeast. According to Obadiah, however, Edom played a key role in helping the Babylonians destroy Jerusalem and sack the temple in 587 BC. That is why they are listed here.

'By the rivers of Babylon' (verse 1)

The description of God's people sitting down in this strange land by the rivers of Babylon and weeping tugs at the heartstrings. In this simple phrase we feel the trauma as they were torn away from everything that they knew: from their land and their homes, their friends and their families, and even from the place where they worshipped God.

SPACE TO DOODLE

Spend some time imagining the emotions of God's people here. What must it have felt like to be ripped out of your home, away from your loved ones and the temple where you worshipped?

'We hung our harps' (verse 2)

Verses 2-3 are fascinating. They appear to refer to the temple musicians, who had brought their instruments with them into captivity but found that away from God's temple they were unable to worship. Their 'captors' and 'tormentors' may or may not have intended to torture them. They may simply have been asking them to sing a Psalm so they could hear it. But the effect was the same. Being asked to sing a song away from the temple compounded their sense of loss and grief.

SPACE TO DOODLE

For the psalmist, singing was closely bound up with worship. For some people today, however, singing is much less important. How important is singing to you in worship?

QUITE INTERESTING

One of the major roles in temple worship was, as we have seen in numerous Psalms, the playing of music. The Levites, in addition to being gatekeepers and temple guards, were the temple musicians. The reference here to hanging up their harps implies that those singing this Psalm were Levites.

Remember Jerusalem (verses 4-6)

These verses speak powerfully about how determined the psalmist is never to forget Jerusalem. If he forgets, he wishes for two things:

- that his right hand will no longer be able to strum the lyre;

- that his tongue will no longer be able to sing the Psalms.

In other words, for the psalmist, music is bound up tightly with worship in Jerusalem. If he forgets Jerusalem, all ability to worship will be gone forever.

TO THINK ABOUT . . .

What do you need in order to be able to worship God? What is your equivalent of 'Jerusalem', which helps you worship?

'Happy is the one . . .' (verse 9)

The ending of Psalm 137 is one of the most troubling in the whole Psalter, in which the psalmist calls for revenge on the Babylonians and Edomites in graphic and horrifying ways.

> **TO THINK ABOUT . . .**
>
> Spend some time reflecting on verses 7-9. Have you ever felt this angry about something? How does reading the psalmist's expression of anger make you feel? Do you think it is justified here or not?

A separate question is what we do with these verses in public worship. Should we use them or bracket them out? If you were to use them, would you want to say anything before or after?

Now go back and read the Psalm again slowly. Make a note this time of the words that you notice. Are they the same or have they changed? As you finish your reflection on the Psalm, you might like to ask yourself three questions.

- How did it make me feel?
- What did it make me think about?
- What do I now need to pray for/about?

Psalm 139

Psalm 139 is the second of a small collection of eight Psalms (138–45) 'of David' that can be found towards the end of the Psalter. It is a popular Psalm, not least because it reflects deeply on God's knowledge of and care for us, noting that there is nowhere that we can flee from God's presence and no thought that we can have that God does not already know. The majority of the Psalm (verses 1-18 and 23-4) is gentle and cheerful, celebrating the closeness that exists between God and the psalmist. This makes the change of tone in verses 19-22 even more shocking than it might otherwise have been, when the psalmist suddenly turns in condemnation of his enemies.

One of the most beautiful sections of the Psalm talks about God creating us – knitting us together – in our mother's womb. God's care for each one of us begins even before we take our first breath and continues for the rest of our lives.

 Read the Psalm slowly. What words or phrases jump out at you?

Psalm 139
For the director of music. Of David. A psalm

¹ You have searched me, LORD,
    and you know me.
² You know when I sit and when I rise;
    you perceive my thoughts from afar.
³ You discern my going out and my lying down;
    you are familiar with all my ways.
⁴ Before a word is on my tongue
    you, LORD, know it completely.
⁵ You hem me in behind and before,
    and you lay your hand upon me.
⁶ Such knowledge is too wonderful for me,
    too lofty for me to attain.

⁷ Where can I go from your Spirit?
    Where can I flee from your presence?
⁸ If I go up to the heavens, you are there;
    if I make my bed in the depths, you are there.
⁹ If I rise on the wings of the dawn,
    if I settle on the far side of the sea,
¹⁰ even there your hand will guide me,
    your right hand will hold me fast.
¹¹ If I say, 'Surely the darkness will hide me
    and the light become night around me,'
¹² even the darkness will not be dark to you;
    the night will shine like the day,
    for darkness is as light to you.

¹³ For you created my inmost being;
    you knit me together in my mother's womb.
¹⁴ I praise you because I am fearfully and wonderfully made;
    your works are wonderful,
    I know that full well.

¹⁵ My frame was not hidden from you
    when I was made in the secret place,
    when I was woven together in the depths of the earth.
¹⁶ Your eyes saw my unformed body;
    all the days ordained for me were written in your book
    before one of them came to be.
¹⁷ How precious to me are your thoughts, God!
    How vast is the sum of them!
¹⁸ Were I to count them,
    they would outnumber the grains of sand –
    when I awake, I am still with you.

¹⁹ If only you, God, would slay the wicked!
    Away from me, you who are bloodthirsty!
²⁰ They speak of you with evil intent;
    your adversaries misuse your name.
²¹ Do I not hate those who hate you, Lord,
    and abhor those who are in rebellion against you?
²² I have nothing but hatred for them;
    I count them my enemies.
²³ Search me, God, and know my heart;
    test me and know my anxious thoughts.
²⁴ See if there is any offensive way in me,
    and lead me in the way everlasting.

STANDING BACK
Looking at the whole Psalm

The Psalm falls into four distinct sections, beginning with God's knowledge of us, then moving on, in the second section, to the impossibility of escaping God's presence. The third section reflects on God's knowledge of us from birth, and the fourth turns, as we noted above, to a somewhat violent condemnation of the wicked.

TO THINK ABOUT . . .

Look at the four different sections of the Psalm (verses 1-6, 7-12, 13-18, 19-24). What title would you give to each section and what is the main focus of each? You might like to jot down the words from each section that you feel capture it best.

Section 1 (verses 1-6)

Section 2 (verses 7-12)

Section 3 (verses 13-18)

Section 4 (verses 19-24)

As we noted above, verses 19-22 are a shocking part of the Psalm, and they are even more shocking because they seem to come from nowhere and disappear again equally fast.

- Some people think that verses 19-22 are the core purpose of the whole Psalm – the psalmist is reminding God how well he knows him and that he (the psalmist) is in the right whereas his enemies are not.

- Others think that these verses do not fit with the rest of the Psalm at all, which is a gentle reflection of the closeness between God and the psalmist, and have been added in later.

TO THINK ABOUT . . .

Spend some time thinking about these verses. Do you think they fit? What do you think the Psalm is about?

ZOOMING IN
Picking up some details

The title

This Psalm is one of the many said to be 'of David' – either written by him or dedicated to him. Either way, the title 'of David' invites us to locate it in the context of his life.

TO THINK ABOUT . . .

Consider this Psalm in the context of David. How might it fit into what you know about him and his life? Is there a particular time in his life that you can imagine him singing it? If you are in need of inspiration, look at 1 Samuel 16:1-13; 18:1-30; 2 Samuel 11:1–12:25; 18:6–19:8; 1 Kings 2:10-12.

'You know me' (verse 1)

The word 'know' occurs six times in the Psalm (verses 1, 2, 4, 6, 14 and 23), alongside other words that also communicate God's knowledge of us.

TO THINK ABOUT . . .

Spend some time noting all the words connected with God's knowledge of us. Reflect on what that tells you about God and about yourself. How does this depth of knowledge make you feel?

'Where can I go?' (verse 7)

The idea of verses 7-12 is that there is nowhere on earth or under the earth that is outside God's love and presence. The word translated 'presence' in verse 7 literally means 'face'. In a way, these verses are a reflection on what it would be like to play hide-and-seek with God – an impossible task because there is nowhere, high or low, far or near, that can escape God's gaze.

TO THINK ABOUT . . .

Think about the description of hiding from God. Are you hiding from God in any area of life right now?

'You knit me together' (verse 13)

Verses 13-16 are an in-depth reflection on the human body and human identity. It is a remarkable meditation on human worth in the eyes of God.

SPACE TO DOODLE

Allow the words of verses 13-16 to sink in. Jot down the words/ideas that come to you while you think about your body in these terms. What do you think of your body – can you say with the psalmist that you are 'fearfully and wonderfully made'?

QUITE INTERESTING

The Hebrew word translated 'knit' more commonly means 'to weave together'. The image is a lovely one of God weaving us into life. It is interesting that our common idiom for this kind of idea today comes from an allied but contrasting 'homecraft' – not weaving but knitting.

'How precious to me are your thoughts' (verse 17)

Verses 17-18 make a short doxology or hymn of praise to God at the end of this longer praise section about God's knowledge of us. The word for 'thoughts' is the same word as the one used in verse 2 ('you perceive my thoughts from afar'). God's thoughts, in contrast to our own which can be seen from far off, are weighty and countless.

TO THINK ABOUT ...

What do you think the psalmist is talking about when he speaks of God's thoughts? What kind of thoughts do you associate with God?

'Know my anxious thoughts' (verse 23)

The word for 'thoughts' used in verse 23 is a different one from the one used in verses 2 and 17. That word refers to anything at all that you might think about, dark or troubled thoughts, those that disquiet or upset you. Here, the psalmist invites God to explore these thoughts and decide if they are wicked or not. If we count verses 19-22 as part of the Psalm, we could assume that he means these thoughts too. This suggests that there is nothing wrong with being angry.

SPACE TO DOODLE

Reflect on your own 'troubled thoughts'. What form do they take? Would you be confident enough to ask God to search them and decide whether they are wicked or not?

Now go back and read the Psalm again slowly. Make a note this time of the words that you notice. Are they the same or have they changed? As you finish your reflection on the Psalm, you might like to ask yourself three questions:

- How did it make me feel?

- What did it make me think about?

- What do I now need to pray for/about?

....
....
....
....
....
....
....
....
....
....
....
....
....
....
....
....
....
....
....
....
....
....
....

Psalm 145

Psalm 145 is the last in the 'David collection' (Psalms 138–45) and comes before the five final doxological or praising Psalms that end the Psalter. In many ways, it bears a closer resemblance to the doxological Psalms than it does to the other Psalms in the David collection since it is an extended reflection on praising God and why we do it. Within the Jewish tradition, Psalm 145 is one of the most prayed of all the Psalms.

The Talmud (a collection of sayings by Jewish rabbis) declares that Psalm 145 should be prayed three times a day (Talmud Berakhot 4b). This presents a challenge for many people today. Should we pray a relentlessly cheerful Psalm even when we feel the opposite of cheerful? It highlights something important about the spiritual discipline of thankfulness – a discipline that does not in any way diminish the hard times in our lives but focuses us on giving thanks to God for who God is, even when we do not feel like it.

 Read the Psalm slowly. What words or phrases jump out at you?

Psalm 145

A psalm of praise. Of David.

¹ I will exalt you, my God the King;
   I will praise your name for ever and ever.
² Every day I will praise you
   and extol your name for ever and ever.

³ Great is the LORD and most worthy of praise;
   his greatness no one can fathom.
⁴ One generation commends your works to another;
   they tell of your mighty acts.
⁵ They speak of the glorious splendour of your majesty –
   and I will meditate on your wonderful works.
⁶ They tell of the power of your awesome works –
   and I will proclaim your great deeds.
⁷ They celebrate your abundant goodness
   and joyfully sing of your righteousness.

⁸ The LORD is gracious and compassionate,
   slow to anger and rich in love.

⁹ The LORD is good to all;
   he has compassion on all he has made.
¹⁰ All your works praise you, LORD;
   your faithful people extol you.
¹¹ They tell of the glory of your kingdom
   and speak of your might,
¹² so that all people may know of your mighty acts
   and the glorious splendour of your kingdom.
¹³ Your kingdom is an everlasting kingdom,
   and your dominion endures through all generations.

The LORD is trustworthy in all he promises
   and faithful in all he does.

¹⁴ The LORD upholds all who fall
    and lifts up all who are bowed down.
¹⁵ The eyes of all look to you,
    and you give them their food at the proper time.
¹⁶ You open your hand
    and satisfy the desires of every living thing.

¹⁷ The LORD is righteous in all his ways
    and faithful in all he does.
¹⁸ The LORD is near to all who call on him,
    to all who call on him in truth.
¹⁹ He fulfils the desires of those who fear him;
    he hears their cry and saves them.
²⁰ The LORD watches over all who love him,
    but all the wicked he will destroy.

²¹ My mouth will speak in praise of the LORD.
    Let every creature praise his holy name
    for ever and ever.

STANDING BACK
Looking at the whole Psalm

Psalm 145 is an acrostic Psalm, with each verse beginning with the next letter of the alphabet (or, more accurately, because it is Hebrew, the *alephbet*). There are twenty-two letters in the Hebrew *alephbet* as vowels are not included, but you will notice that there are only twenty-one verses. This is because one letter is missed out – the 'n' or *nun*. It is not clear why this is!

TO THINK ABOUT . . .

Knowing that the psalmist worked hard on the structure of the Psalm, spend time focusing on that and see what you notice about it. Does anything strike you about how the Psalm is put together?

QUITE INTERESTING

Verses 11-13 focus on God's kingdom. In the acrostic poem these verses begin with k – l – m respectively. The Hebrew for 'king' is *melek*. It is likely that the psalmist chose the three verses whose first letters spelled out *melek* backwards deliberately as the place in the Psalm to reflect on God's 'kingdom'.

This Psalm explores the idea of praise. Throughout the Psalm there are decisions to praise ('I will exalt you'), statements that praise will happen ('they tell of your mighty acts') and reasons given for praise happening ('Great is the LORD and most worthy of praise'). Sometimes the word 'praise' is used; at other times different words are used.

TO THINK ABOUT . . .

In the Psalm, there are so many different words for praising God, so many different ways that they went about doing it. Go through the Psalm and jot down:

- the different words used that, when put together, all point to praise of God;

- the different types of praise (decisions to praise; statements of praise; reasons for praise; any others you notice).

ZOOMING IN
Picking up some details

The title

As with Psalm 139, the title of this Psalm invites us to associate it with David and the events of his life. The title suggests that, in this Psalm, David led not just the Israelites but also the whole of creation in praise of God. Praise is a key feature in the Psalms, an action that recognises God's nature and gives thanks for all that God has done.

TO THINK ABOUT . . .

This is a Psalm of praise from beginning to end. If you were to follow the instruction from the Talmud to pray this three times a day, what impact might it have on you?

'My God the King' (verse 1)

God's kingship is referred to regularly throughout the Psalms, but there are only two places (here and Psalm 98:6) where God is addressed as 'the King'. Kings were all powerful in the ancient world and considered to be the owners of all the lands that fell within their kingdoms. This was one of the reasons that the prophet Samuel was so opposed to Israel having a king – Israel was set up differently, with each of the twelve tribes owning a portion of the land that God had given them. In Israel, the king held everything in trust for God the true King.

SPACE TO DOODLE

What does it mean to you to call God 'King'?

God is . . . (verses 3-9)

Verses 3-9 contain a list of descriptions of God from 'great'
(verse 3) to 'good' in (verse 9). Woven between these
descriptions are phrases that tell of what God has done for his
people (works, acts, etc.). This is important. Throughout the
Bible, 'who God is' is linked closely with 'what God has done';
we know who God is because of what he has done for us. It is
striking that there are so many different words used to describe
God's 'works'. These different words all contribute to the
sense that God's action – what God has done for him – is very
important for the psalmist.

TO THINK ABOUT . . .

Jot down on one side of the box the different descriptions
of God ('great', etc.) in verses 3-9, and on the other side
list the words that describe what God has done. Spend
some time reflecting on the words used. What words
would you add from your own experience?

'Your works praise you' (verse 10)

The psalmist notes that it is not just human beings who praise God but also the whole of the created world. 'Your works' in verses 10 appears to refer to everything that had been created by God: human beings and animals, plants and trees.

SPACE TO DOODLE

How does creation praise God? Might this inform our own praise of God?

QUITE INTERESTING

As mentioned in our reflection on Psalm 118, one of the most important words in the Old Testament – and in the Psalter – is the Hebrew word *ḥeṣed*, which is translated as 'steadfast love' or 'loving kindness'. It is hard to translate into English as it has a range of meanings covering love towards God and towards human beings as well as faithfulness and steadfastness. The phrase 'your faithful people' in verse 10 translates from 'your *ḥeṣed* people' – 'loving and steadfast, kind and faithful'.

'The Lord is trustworthy in all he promises' (verses 13b-20)

In many ways, verses 13-20 and 3-9 complement each other, since they return to the theme of who God is as revealed in what God has done.

TO THINK ABOUT . . .

Look through verses 13b-20 and jot down all the different descriptions of God's trustworthiness and the evidence given for this.

When you have done that, compare your list with what you picked out from verses 3-9. What is the same and what is different?

Now go back and read the Psalm again slowly. Make a note this time of the words that you notice. Are they the same or have they changed? As you finish your reflection on the Psalm, you might like to ask yourself three questions:

- How did it make me feel?

- What did it make me think about?

- What do I now need to pray for/about?

....
....
....
....
....
....
....
....
....
....
....
....
....
....
....
....
....
....
....
....
....
....

Psalm 150

As well as being the very last Psalm in the Psalter, Psalm 150 is the last of five praise or *hallel* Psalms. Each of these Psalms (Psalm 146–50) begins with 'Praise the LORD', but Psalm 150 uses the word 'praise' thirteen times from beginning to end. As well as being noticeable for its use of the word 'praise', Psalm 150 is strikingly concise, expressing its praise in six short but powerful verses.

Just as Psalm 1 begins the Psalter so well by reflecting on the life of a person who delights in the law of the Lord, so Psalm 150 ends with a final shout (or indeed shouts) of praise. A life lived as Psalm 1 lays out will, over time, lead to the praise of God we find in Psalm 150, even if on the way we pass through the darkest valleys and the deepest pits of despair. As such, Psalm 1 and 150 are appropriate bookends to the Psalter.

 Read the Psalm slowly. What words or phrases jump out at you?

Psalm 150

[1] Praise the LORD.

Praise God in his sanctuary;
    praise him in his mighty heavens.
[2] Praise him for his acts of power;
    praise him for his surpassing greatness.
[3] Praise him with the sounding of the trumpet,
    praise him with the harp and lyre,
[4] praise him with tambourine and dancing,
    praise him with the strings and pipe,
[5] praise him with the clash of cymbals,
    praise him with resounding cymbals.

[6] Let everything that has breath praise the LORD.

Praise the LORD.

STANDING BACK
Looking at the whole Psalm

Psalm 150 falls into three sections:

- Verses 1-2 set out not only where God is to be praised but also the reasons for it.

- Verses 3-5 describe how God is to be praised – with all the musical instruments to be used.

- Verse 6 expresses the wish that every living creature might praise God and returns to the command to praise the Lord.

TO THINK ABOUT . . .

Look at the three sections of the Psalm. What effect do these three sections have on you as you read? You might find yourself inspired by them, or feel that, overall, the Psalm is a bit loud; you might feel caught up in the praise, or find it tiring.

The word *hallelujah* is Hebrew for 'praise the Lord'. *Hallelu* is a plural command and *Yah* the shortened form of the divine name *YHWH*. This Psalm, then, begins and ends with a command to praise the Lord. In between these two commands are given reasons for the praise and a description of how it should be done.

SPACE TO DOODLE

The word *hallelujah* and the phrase 'praise the Lord' are the Hebrew and English version of the same thing.

Do they feel the same to you? Or slightly different?

ZOOMING IN
Picking up some details

'Praise God in ...' (verse 1)

The opening verse identifies where God is when we praise him – in his sanctuary or holy place, in his mighty heavens. The two words are not intended to indicate two different places – the temple was thought to open directly into heaven and vice versa. What is important is that God is to be praised both in the temple and in the created world that he has made.

> **TO THINK ABOUT ...**
>
> Where do you praise God most easily?

QUITE INTERESTING

The phrase translated 'heavens' is the Hebrew word *raqia*, which means a solid, thin expanse and refers to the dome of the sky that Hebrew thinkers believed held back the waters they thought flowed above the sky. The psalmist then commands us to praise God where he lives above the sky.

'Praise him for . . .' (verse 2)

Verse 2 turns our attention to why we praise God: because of his acts of power (i.e. what he has done) and because of his surpassing greatness (i.e. who he is). In other words, the psalmist gives us two headings that remind us of the need to praise God.

TO THINK ABOUT . . .

If you were to write down your reasons for praise, what would you list under the heading, 'What God has done'?

What would you list under the heading, 'Who God is'?

'Praise him with . . .' (verses 3-5)

The next three verses describe the instruments to be used for praising God:

- trumpet: in Hebrew, the *shofar*. It was made from animal horn and was not melodic. Instead, it summoned God's people to worship;

- harp: an ancient stringed instrument with ten strings, designed to accompany singing;

- lyre: an ancient stringed instrument with seven or eight strings, also designed to accompany singing;

- tambourine: a frame drum normally played by women. The drum would have been held in the left hand and struck with the right to accompany dancing;

- strings: probably a lute, often played by wandering prophets;

- pipe: probably some kind of flute;

- cymbals: there are two kinds of cymbals referred to, one that makes something like a clanging sound, and the other more of a clashing sound.

TO THINK ABOUT . . .

What might this praise of God have sounded like? Why do you think the psalmist suggests so many different instruments? If you were to translate these instruments into modern worship, what instruments might you list here?

'Let everything that has breath' (verse 6)

The importance of praising God is emphasised by the final verse of the Psalm. The very purpose of having breath is so that we can praise God. As a result, everything that has breath should put it to its intended use in praising God. It is a fitting end to the whole Psalter. The purpose of all living things created by God is to reflect God's glory and honour back to their creator. The way we do this is in praise.

SPACE TO DOODLE

If you were to praise God right now, what would you say?

Now go back and read the Psalm again slowly. Make a note this time of the words that you notice. Are they the same or have they changed? As you finish your reflection on the Psalm, you might like to ask yourself three questions:

- How did it make me feel?
- What did it make me think about?
- What do I now need to pray for/about?

....
....
....
....
....
....
....
....
....
....
....
....
....
....
....
....
....
....
....
....
....
....

HODDER & STOUGHTON

Hodder & Stoughton is the UK's
leading Christian publisher,
with a wide range of books from
the bestselling authors in the UK
and around the world ranging from
Christian lifestyle and theology to
apologetics, testimony and fiction.
We also publish the world's
most popular Bible translation
in modern English, the New
International Version, renowned
for its accuracy and readability.

Hodderfaith.com   Hodderbibles.co.uk
@HodderFaith   /HodderFaith

Discover more journalling resources from Hodder & Stoughton

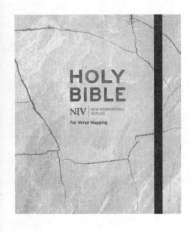

NIV Bible for Journalling and
Verse-Mapping: Kintsugi
In addition to wide, blank margins for
journalling, this edition is interspersed
with 32 pages introducing the art of
verse-mapping.
9781473680548
Hardback | £27.99

NIV Journalling Black Hardback Bible
With wide, ruled margins, this Bible is perfect
for readers who love to add their own notes,
references and personal reflections alongside
the text.
9781529353624
Hardback | £24.99

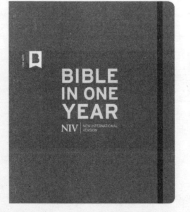

NIV Journalling Bible in One Year: Red
A reading plan designed to help you read
the whole Bible in one year, with wide
margins for adding your thoughts as you go.
9781473674967
Hardback | £24.99